The Illness That We Are

J. G. Dehmer

Marie-Louise von Franz, Honorary Patron

**Studies in Jungian Psychology
by Jungian Analysts**

Daryl Sharp, General Editor

The Illness
That We Are

A Jungian Critique of Christianity

John P. Dourley

Canadian Cataloguing in Publication Data

Dourley, John P.
   The illness that we are

(Studies in Jungian psychology by Jungian analysts; 17)

Includes index.

ISBN 0-919123-16-3

1. Christianity—Controversial literature.
2. Jung, C. G. (Carl Gustav), 1875-1961.   3. Whole
and parts (Psychology).   4. Psychology and religion.
I. Title.   II. Series.

BR121.2.D68 1984   230   C84-099181-9

INNER CITY BOOKS
Box 1271, Station Q, Toronto, Canada M4T 2P4
Telephone (416) 927-0355

Honorary Patron: Marie-Louise von Franz.
Publisher and General Editor: Daryl Sharp.
Editorial Board: Fraser Boa, Daryl Sharp, Marion Woodman.

INNER CITY BOOKS was founded in 1980 to promote the
understanding and practical application of the work of C.G. Jung.

Cover: The brazen serpent of Moses on the cross, analogous to the
alchemical *serpens mercurialis* (Eleazar, *Uraltes chymisches Werk,* 1760).
In alchemy, the fiery spirit of Mercurius was seen as the compensation for
the lofty spirit of Christ (see below, pp. 33-34, 97).

Photo page 6 by Karsh of Ottawa.

Illustration page 22: Pen and ink drawing (Publisher's Collection).

Illustration page 70 from *C.G. Jung: Word and Image* (Bollingen Series
XCVII:2), ed. Aniela Jaffé (Princeton: Princeton University Press, 1979).

Index by Daryl Sharp

Printed and bound in Canada by Webcom Limited.

Contents

See final pages for descriptions of other Inner City Books

Jung in his study, at the age of 85

1

Jung's Ambivalence Toward Christianity

> *In its religious attitude ... the West is extraverted.
> ... Extraversion ... cannot credit man with a
> psyche which contains anything not imported into
> it from outside, either by human teaching or divine
> grace. From this point of view it is downright
> blasphemy to assert that man has it in him to
> accomplish his own redemption. Nothing in our
> religion encourages the idea of the self-liberating
> power of the mind.*
> —C.G. Jung[1]

The psychology of C.G. Jung is currently gaining widespread
and sympathetic acceptance in Christian circles. Those concerned with the recovery of a revitalized Christian spirituality
and theology quite rightly point to central themes in Jung's
thought which describe humanity as endowed in its core with
a sense of the ultimate—the divine as well as the demonic.
Indeed, Jung's psychology does rest ultimately on a belief in
the reality of archetypal energies transcendent to the ego
which, when they hold it in their grip, convince the ego of the
truth and power of deity and devil alike.

Jung discerned in the movement of these energies a drive
toward wholeness, understood as a progressive unification of
one's many disparate components, always carrying with it an
ever more extensive empathy with the world beyond one's
individual life. This he called the process of individuation.
Jung came to equate the experience of one's wholeness with
the experience of God, and to see its expression in certain
transpersonal and transcultural symbols of the deity.

Christians wishing to appropriate the spirit of Jung's insights in the service of the revitalization of their own tradition

rightly appreciate the value Jung places on wholeness (rather than perfection) as the goal of maturation, as well as the lively sense of the interior life that permeates so much of his thought. They too would like to think of this movement toward wholeness as God's intent for humanity. They correctly perceive that an intellectual-theological recovery of an anthropology which would locate the divine-human encounter within the psyche might well lead those concerned with a vital spiritual life to a more immediate and intense experience of God as a whole-making power rooted in life's depths. After all, it is difficult to take the interior life seriously if it has been abruptly dismissed by one's religious tradition as a meeting place of God and the human.

Those moving to incorporate Jung's psychology in a Christian framework may also be impressed by the reverence in which Jung holds symbolic and mythical expression. They may be aware of his contention that all powerful and religious symbols arise from a common human source and depth, which he called the collective unconscious, to which each individual continues to have access in the pursuit of his or her spiritual life. An experience of this level of one's own humanity could intensify one's appreciation of all symbolism as well as the reality from which symbols come and to which they point. Further, an enhanced sensitivity to symbolic experience in general might very well lead to a heightened experience of those symbols specific to the Christian tradition.

As such a consciousness developed, Christian symbols would no longer be understood as foreign or "revealed" pieces of information about divine realms and realities wholly beyond the human, nor as referents to discrete historical intrusions of the divine into human affairs separated from the present by space and time. Rather they could be experienced as expressions of the deepest rhythms and movements of psychic and spiritual life, enabling the individual more easily to enter and more fully to be transformed by these rhythms. In this case the symbols and myths on which particular religious faiths are based would reveal the powers of transformation of those levels of psychic and spiritual life which transcend the ego, working to heal and make it whole in the here and now.

In such a context Jung understands the Christian myth to be a great gift to humanity. A more thorough consideration of the totality of Jung's thought, however, reveals also the elements of a continued and consistent criticism of Christianity. Indeed, he challenges believers to transcend its limitations in the interests of their personal health, as well as in the wider interests of the movement of historical consciousness to a plane more capable of preserving humanity from self-destruction. In short, Jung's undoubted appreciation of the psycho-spiritual potentialities inherent in the Christian myth is qualified by an equally keen perception of its shortcomings.

Because of this ambivalence it is useful to examine those foundational elements in Jung's thought not easily reconcilable with mainstream Christian orthodoxies. For instance, already mentioned is Jung's clearly stated location of the genesis of religious experience—and so of the Christian God as well as all the pagan Gods and Goddesses—*within the human psyche,* even if beyond the ego's manipulation or control.[2] To take this side of Jung's thought seriously entails a radical conception of divine immanence, or at least the acceptance of a religious epistemology which would be more candid in its admission that humanity's experience of divinity derives from an in-depth experience of itself. The possibility of a deity-engendering faculty within the psyche is understandably a threat to a Christianity still largely committed to living under the burden of its religious projections understood for the most part literally and historically.

Jung's conception of a relatively autonomous unconscious inexorably giving birth, through human consciousness, to a plethora of deities throughout the history of mankind also raises problems related to the relativity of such an outpouring of epiphanies. If humanity not only can but must create its Gods and Goddesses, as Jung believes, then the possibility of any one of them being the absolute and exhaustive expression of humanity's deity-engendering capacity would appear to be rather slim. The idea that the experience of the divine is due to archetypal activity native to the psyche certainly modifies, if it does not render entirely premature and adolescent, claims to absolute and exhaustive revelations which have somehow drained the unconscious of its ability to express its religious energies in future revelations. Such a final Word would seem to block rather than stimulate further and fuller statements from the unconscious.

The spirit that guided Jung's investigation would contend that the truth of any one God's or Goddess's revelation can be most fully and effectively comprehended against the background of the families of other Gods and Goddesses to which other cultures and individuals have ascribed a "final" revelation. In various of his letters, for instance, Jung refers to the figure of Jesus as one expression of the Self, and relates the Jesus myth to the Osiris myth; to the Son of Man in the Book of Enoch; to the Buddha, Hindu philosophy, Taoism and the mystical side of the Islamic tradition; and to the Anthropos myth. He also relates the historical figure of Jesus, and the projections he attracted, to the historical figures of the Buddha, Confucius, Lao-Tse and Pythagoras (though he allows that the projections onto the latter figures were not as powerful as those attracted by Jesus).[3]

This view implies that only through an understanding of the variations of any particular revelation or myth can that which lies behind them and seeks expression through them be understood. In this conception of humanity's diverse revelatory experiences, a final revelation becomes some kind of eschatological and distant consciousness in which the limitations of discrete and currently competing revelations are transcended toward a non-coercive and more inclusive wealth—to which all enduring specific revelations would no doubt make their significant but partial contributions.

On this side of such an idealized but conceptually inescapable state of mind, where humanity currently lives and moves and has its being, any claims to a final revelation appear as forced constrictions to the development of a more adequate religious consciousness. One suspects also that these claimants to finality remain unaware of, or are incapable of discerning, the functional equivalents in humanity's experience elsewhere. Thus the full price of the revitalization and broadening of the human spirit attached to Jung's challenging understanding of the human psyche and its religious propensities may ultimately prove to be too high for an individual or community clinging to its no doubt God-given, but partial, revelation as final, unique and all-encompassing.

The problem sketched here is particularly acute among the world's current reigning monotheisms: Christianity, Judaism and Islam. Here three distinct and transcendent Gods with three distinct revelations—each with absolute claims to universal implementation as the condition of humanity's salvation, and with immense numbers of devotees—face each other in a shrinking globe with obviously increasing enmity. Though this enmity may be less evident (though not always) in their sacred texts and interpretive theologies, the loss of life attendant upon these faiths, reported almost daily in the media, should make this enmity impossible to be concealed any longer, even from the eyes of faith.

In the face of this problem, Christianity, with its central symbol of death and resurrection, could be the candidate among the monotheisms to break this impasse and to affirm itself by transcending itself—to die in its present configuration in order to rise in some form of more inclusive consciousness. It might do this by coming to see itself as one, but only one, significant and very valuable realization in history of the psyche's drive to express the full extent of its religious import. It could then more humbly confess its partiality and seek missing aspects of its potential wholeness in the religious experience of other traditions, or in direct dialogue with the source of all religious experience—the unconscious within each individual.

In this sense, Jung's challenge to the Christian, and by extension to any believer in a final revelation, may be to lose a lesser faith in the interests of a greater, more inclusive one.

In Jung's view such an option would be supported, perhaps even demanded, by the psyche as generator of historical religious consciousness; for he sees the movement toward such an extended consciousness as incarnating the deepest movement of the psyche's energies. The alternative would seem to be a continued adherence to a once enlivening but now possibly fatal myth.

A more somber note in Jung's thought implies that this option is one which humanity itself will have to face if it is not to be destroyed by one or another of its "saving" revelations. For even though these revelations are now more widely experienced as constricting in themselves, they continue to manifest the gripping power of archetypal possession, enabling them to induce a commitment en masse which would only too gladly eliminate, by conversion or extermination, all counter-commitments—that is, other faiths and beliefs which, themselves vested with the awesome powers of conviction arising from the unconscious, contend with equal single-mindedness for possession of the individual and collective mind.

Any sustained reflection on the major themes in Jung's life and work brings these questions to mind. It may therefore be of some help to the religious and Christian mind to bring into a higher relief that apparent ambivalence in Jung's writings which can be so admiring of the Christian tradition, its symbols and its rites, yet also accuse it of currently making people ill. A closer examination of this apparent flat contradiction in Jung's mind reveals, I believe, an underlying consistency—an attitude that not only challenges the current Christian standpoint, but offers a hope to humanity far beyond anything at present available through any single religious tradition.

2

Sacrosanct Unintelligibility

I have to ask myself also, in all seriousness, whether it might not be far more dangerous if Christian symbols were made inaccessible to thoughtful understanding by being banished to a sphere of sacrosanct unintelligibility. They can easily become so remote from us that their irrationality turns into preposterous nonsense.
— C.G. Jung[4]

The religious apologetic, or apology for religion, that abounds in Jung's work is related to his analysis of the deplorable state of both religion and the healing arts of his time. He was convinced that the proper function of religion, as of depth psychology, was to provide access to those energies which renewed one's life by making it more whole, both personally and in relation to the wider community.

In Jung's view, the psychological experience of unconscious compensation, which demonstrably moves toward wholeness, is comparable to the experience of God; indeed, he argues that the two are virtually indistinguishable. The experience of this wholeness or psychic integration Jung came to equate with the concept of grace:

A very modern form of psychology—"analytical" or "complex" psychology—envisages the possibility of there being certain processes in the unconscious which, by virtue of their symbolism, compensate the defects and anfractuosities of the conscious attitude. When these unconscious compensations are made conscious through the analytical technique, they produce such a change in the conscious attitude that we are entitled to speak of a new level of consciousness. The method cannot, however, produce the actual process of unconscious compensation; for that we depend upon the unconscious psyche or the "grace of God"—names make no difference.[5]

With this understanding Jung could take the position that the source of healing and the origin of religious experience were one, internal to the human and of such a nature that the true practitioner of medicine and the true educer of religious experience must participate in each other's endeavors—because both draw ultimately on a common source in the depths of the human psyche. Much of Jung's criticism of both religious and medical therapy, therefore, was grounded in his conviction that the modern healing arts and the mainstream Western Christian tradition had severed themselves from the healing, that is whole-making, energies of the psyche.

Medicine had become a technology, a "rational" technique. Religion had become the domain of a "sacrosanct unintelligibility" and thus "preposterous nonsense" for much the same reason. By adopting a purely rationalistic approach to its role as mediator of the Word of God and of grace, it too had become technologized—the Word of God had been reduced to mere wordiness through the rational categories used in its theological interpretation. The means of grace had thus come to be conceived too much like any other form of productivity. Religion had lost its ear for the symbolic language spoken by healing and religious energies, and so had largely lost contact with the energies themselves. In short, religion was cut off from its own origins in the human psyche precisely through its concoction of rationalistic, interpretive theologies perversely designed to miss, often with unerring methodological consistency, the point and substance of the myth and symbol to which they were applied.

Confronted with this situation Jung was forced to enter the theological arena in an effort to discover how a myth which purported to give life, in fact so often proved pathogenic in the lives of those striving to find some meaning in it. Jung's attention to matters theological, then, initially prompted by his concern as a healer, took the form of progressively showing throughout his creative years how the major truths currently lost in "sacrosanct unintelligibility" were in fact statements of the deepest movements of the human psyche toward its human and humanizing maturation. In his essay on the Trinity, for instance, he writes:

> To many people it may seem strange that a doctor with a scientific training should interest himself in the Trinity at all. But anyone who has experienced how closely and meaningfully these *représentations collectives* are bound up with the weal and woe of the human soul will readily understand that the central symbol of Christianity must have, above all else, a psychological meaning, for without this it could never have acquired any universal meaning whatever, but would have been relegated long ago to the dusty cabinet of spiritual monstrosities and shared the fate of the many-armed and many-headed gods of India and Greece.[6]

Admittedly, Jung's analysis of institutionalized Christianity's current remove from the source of spiritual life is at times lacking in perfect theological clarity. Many theologians, for instance, would distinguish between the myth itself—the original and now canonical revelation—and Church dogma as an equally canonical but once-removed collective and conscious reflection on the myth's true meaning. Sometimes Jung misses such distinctions, but the purport of his critique remains unblurred by the absence of these theological niceties. Although he not infrequently uses as synonyms the words dogma, symbol and myth, it is because for Jung any or all of them may describe that peculiar mode of discourse best suited to express humanity's experience of those energies that approach consciousness from the unconscious.[7] By whatever name we may give them, it is through their symbolic and mythical form that these energies retain their powerful capacity to transform, by leading us into the same depths from which they originally emerged into historical consciousness.

To Jung the loss of the symbolic sense was a catastrophe for both individual and society. It meant that the healing and religious disciplines of his time, themselves cut off from their own deepest resources, blocked their practitioners and devotees from them also. The consequences appeared, on an individual level, in the widespread occurrence and experience of meaninglessness, depression and neurosis, and socially in the outbreak of new epidemics of faith (often in political form) as the unconscious offered demonic configurations of mass-mindedness to fill the gaps left by the demise of the traditional religions.

Jung's critique differentiates between the paths taken by Reformed and Roman Christianity in the process of disengaging themselves from the roots of life in the human psyche. Perhaps because of his own Reform heritage he is particularly harsh on that tradition, although he consistently approves of the Reform option for a direct experience of the divine.[8] In particular he feels such experience is of great value in developing a finely tuned moral sense, honed by the absence of easier sacramental relief from guilt offered in other traditions:

> The Protestant is left to God alone. For him there is no confession, no absolution, no possibility of an expiatory *opus divinum* of any kind. . . . But, for this very reason, the Protestant has a unique chance to make himself conscious of sin to a degree that is hardly possible for a Catholic mentality, as confession and absolution are always at hand to ease excess of tension.[9]

But at the same time he is again consistent in his position that the historical development of the Reformation has culminated in a wholly conscious theology, removing humanity from a sense of its divine depths in favor of a much bleaker relation to an entirely transcendent God whose mystery has been rendered unintelligible by the conscious categories brought to the interpretation of his revelation.[10] In this respect he sees the Reform tradition as "really and truly nailed fast to the Patriarchal line of the Old Testament," unhealthily removed from the essentially maternal and feminine experience that is inseparable from immediate contact with the unconscious as generator of religious experience.[11]

For these reasons a significant side of Jung's thought is more favorable to aspects of the Catholic tradition. He values highly its retention of the symbolic, that is the sense of mystery still attached to the symbol, especially in the context of its re-enactment in liturgy and rite. For Jung these expressions and activities are born from the unconscious and so are peculiarly equipped to graciously lead one into an experience of their generating source. He knew the importance of this from his analytic practice:

> I had to go with them [those of his patients with unmediated experience of the unconscious] through the crises of passionate conflicts, through the panics of madness, through desperate confusions and depressions which were grotesque and terrible at the same time, so that I am fully aware of the extraordinary importance of dogma and ritual, at least as methods of mental hygiene.[12]

But whether Jung's view of the nature and function of symbol and rite is compatible with Catholicism's current understanding of them is questionable. A case could certainly be made from Jung's position that, whether or not Catholicism is theologically conscious of what occurs psychologically in symbolic discourse and ritual re-enactment, the configuration Catholicism gives to these activities does afford the Catholic an access to the unconscious denied to practitioners of traditions whose theologies remain unaware of the unconscious or unable to integrate it into their beliefs and practices. From this point of view, the contact with the unconscious provided by and through sacramental activity may be the ultimate justification, though this is not the precise Catholic understanding, of the *ex opere operato,* by which term the more or less automatic effectiveness of the sacrament is "explained."

Jung would thus challenge Catholicism to bring to full theological consciousness the intimacy with the unconscious implied in its sacramental activities, and so to become more aware of what it says and does psychologically when it enters into sacramental modes of behavior. This said, Jung's appreciation of sacramentalism was never so great as to tempt him to join a community still possessed of and by so totalitarian an authority system as Catholicism continues to be.[13]

For these differing reasons Jung charged the major Western Christian traditions with blocking rather than enabling the access of their followers to the life they claimed to mediate. In this climate conceptions of faith are divorced from any experiential basis in humanity's awareness of itself, and become dehumanizing substitutes for the life-giving experience of the unconscious which the symbols express. Of this destructive psycho-spiritual situation Jung writes: "It [theology] proclaims doctrines which nobody understands and demands a faith which nobody can manufacture."[14]

The psychological consequences of such pathological conceptions of faith may take many forms. For instance, the situation can breed a fanaticism designed to block a potentially healing and expanding doubt. Such a doubt would be grounded in the human conviction that, whatever the content of such faith may be, in its current lack of integration with life it remains foreign and therefore hostile both to psychological growth and to life itself:

> People who merely believe and don't think always forget that they continually expose themselves to their own worst enemy: doubt. Wherever belief reigns doubt lurks in the background. But thinking people welcome doubt: it serves them as a valuable stepping-stone to better knowledge.[15]

When and if faith as fanaticism is overcome, the results are not always unqualifiedly beneficial. Patterns of depression and emptiness can follow the loss of whatever solace was previously offered by the so-called faith—though paradoxically the depression may be accompanied by rage at the sacrifices made to the dubious God of such faith and his strident moral demands, now felt to be hostile to fuller expressions of human life and spirit. Victims of "sacrosanct unintelligibility" are thus too often faced with "no-win" options. They can grit their teeth and cling fanatically to a burden of "revealed truth" which finds no experiential resonance in themselves. This splits them between the demands of their faith and the demands of their humanity and potential maturity. Or they are driven, often by inner demands for a fuller and more balanced life, into patterns of denial. In the language of their own impoverished theological options such denial is described as "atheism." Not infrequently this carries with it a lingering guilt for having abandoned what may have been, after all, the one true revelation—all the truer precisely because of its unintelligibility.

The ultimate tragedy of faith as "sacrosanct unintelligibility" is that it makes its own rejection a condition of psychological maturity. Too often this breeds the situation where mature individuals, desperate for a sense of depth in their lives, are hampered in their search for meaning by the difficulties in finding access to those levels of themselves which a healthy religious tradition would ordinarily supply.

Jung saw too many people injured by their religious background to escape the realization that contemporary Christian theologians and apologists were woefully unaware of the unconscious as the seat of religion and therefore a potential source of healing. Consequently they were incapable of appreciating, and so mediating to others, the symbolic and healing import of their own professed faith. Obviously irked at this situation Jung writes, "Even intelligent people no longer understand the value and purpose of symbolical truth, and the spokesmen of religion have failed to deliver an apologetic suited to the spirit of the age."[16] His plea to these "spokesmen" is to become conscious of why humanity finds meaning at all in something as unlikely as symbolic discourse:

> Exclusive appeals to faith are a hopeless *petitio principii*, for it is the manifest improbability of symbolical truth that prevents people from believing in it. Instead of insisting so glibly on the necessity of faith, the theologians, it seems to me, should see what can be done to make this faith possible.... And this can only be achieved by reflecting how it came about in the first place that humanity needed the improbability of religious statements, and what it signifies when a totally different spiritual reality is superimposed on the sensuous and tangible actuality of this world.[17]

Jung's reflections on why humanity seemed universally and at all times driven to "the improbability of religious statements" brought him a radically new understanding of religion and its diverse expressions. He came to see religion in its broadest sense as a natural child of the unconscious, and so conceived of a new, "natural" theology which would view the various improbable statements of faith as referents to psychological movements in the universal processes of human renewal and maturation:

> It would be a regrettable mistake if anybody should take my observations as a kind of proof for the existence of God. They prove only the existence of an archetypal God-image, which to my mind is the most we can assert about God psychologically. But as it is a very important and influential archetype, its relatively frequent occurrence seems to be a noteworthy fact for any *theologia naturalis*.[18]

In this sense Jung radically rethought and reapplied the so-called Vincentian Canon, grounding it in the fabric of human psycho-spiritual life. Vincent of Lerins was an early theologian who set as the norm of belief "that which is believed everywhere, by everyone, always." Jung, in various places in his work, seizes on this phrase as a most fortunate expression of psychological orthodoxy, implying in his use of it that the major themes of all religions, being grounded in the psyche, express the same truths, however variously due to cultural and historical conditions, and that their compelling nature is itself responsible for the *consensus gentium* or general assent to the core of these truths.[19]

With this natural theology and its accompanying hermeneutic Jung spent much of his writing life in what can only be called the search for an apology, both for religion in general and for Christianity, which would be capable of better relating —if indeed it did not fuse—religious experience as traditionally understood and the modern discovery of the movements of psychic energy. Thus he goes to great lengths to show how the major Christian motifs—the Trinity, creation, the fall, the meaning of sacrifice (especially as contained in the Catholic rite of the Mass), death, resurrection and eschatological unities —are all expressions of the deepest vitalities of the psyche seeking historical fulfillment in patterns of individual wholeness and communion.[20] As such, these motifs are as deeply grounded in humanity's experience of itself as are the capacity of its spirit to produce poetry and its sweat glands sweat.

In this position of Jung's, in fact, lies one of the major sources of his ambivalence toward Christianity. From this standpoint he could be consistent in his appreciation of the Christian myth and express grave concern at its current demise because it expressed so powerfully for its age these universal themes. But his very appreciation of it as a powerful concretion of universal potencies renders it relative, for Jung's implication is that its full meaning is more apparent when its likenesses elsewhere in other forms are used to bring its specific importance into higher relief.

Jung's attitude, then, involves a dialectic between the particular actualization of a myth and its universal basis in the psyche—which would inevitably result in a multitude of different expressions in history. Applied to Christianity, such a dialectic could make it possible to more fully appreciate the cultural and historical significance of the myth, while at the same time freeing the Christian mind from the now embarrassing and quite possibly socially dangerous claims to a uniqueness that exhausts the possibilities of the archetype behind the myth.

In this respect Jung's critique of Christianity is already either abrasive or liberating, or both, depending on the individual response, even without his deeper criticisms. These center on the contention that the myth is flawed in itself by a constitutional one-sidedness, which further contributes to the illness that we are.

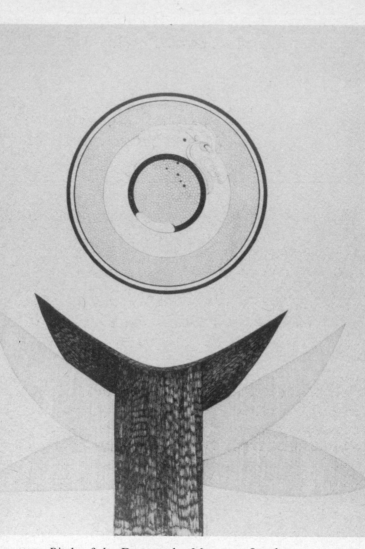

Birth of the Dragon, by Margaret Jacoby.
Snakes and dragons are common representations, in art, dreams
and mythology, of numinous archetypal activity within the psyche, which often demands to be pictured in order to assimilate
the experience.

3

A Systematic Blindness

*What one could almost call a systematic blindness
is simply the effect of the prejudice that God is
outside of man.*
—C.G. Jung[21]

By placing the possibility and necessity of humanity's religious experience in the processes of archetypal activity within the psyche, Jung identifies the archetypes as humanity's God-makers and faith-givers. Most Western theologies identify God not only as the source of revelation but also as the author of the faith in that which is revealed. Thus faith or the grace of belief, as well as what is believed in, is placed well beyond the potentially manipulative grasp of the individual ego.

Jung's psychology is thoroughly steeped in a similar perception, but on an *intrapsychic* basis. He attributes faith (in whatever God or Goddess) to the ego's being gripped and held by the numinous power of the archetype functioning beyond the ego's controlling grasp. Thus in the matter of the priority of the divine in addressing the human, Jung's view sacrifices nothing to traditional conceptions of the divine initiative in revelatory and salvational approaches to humanity. Where he does deviate, however, is in his conception of the transcendent but intrapsychic genesis of both the revelation and the capacity to believe or be forced to believe in it. Those unaware of this inner deity revealing itself from the depths of the soul— and this would include the vast majority of Christian theologians—are, for Jung, suffering from "a systematic blindness."

Where the spirit of Jung's psychology digresses even further from the thrust of most Western theologies is in its invitation, sometimes proferred with a certain urgency, to the believer in any tradition to become more aware of the inner origin and power of his or her reigning divinity. Given this awareness of the direction from which the Gods and Goddesses address humanity, the believer might dialogue more fruitfully with them in order to strike a new covenant or testament more adequate to the needs of one's personal and immediate development, and by extension more in accord with the interests of humanity itself.

As already stated, Jung believes that the intent of the divine power addressing humanity through the unconscious is personal wholeness in interplay with wider empathies. This would be the "divine plan" of the unconscious for humanity. Further, according to Jung a refusal to accept this proferred invitation to higher or broader consciousness can be met with the same vengeful destructiveness that savage Gods of old were wont to wreak on those who opposed their divine injunctions:

> If the demand for self-knowledge is willed by fate and is refused, this negative attitude may end in real death. . . . The unconscious has a thousand ways of snuffing out a meaningless existence.[22]

By thus locating the human capacity and necessity for a sense of the divine in the numinosity of archetypal experience, Jung vests his psychology with a sacramentalism and a sense of the sacred more deeply rooted in humanity than even the sacramental tradition within Christianity can easily tolerate. This is so because of the rather strange intellectual exercises most theologies must go through in order to justify the ecclesiastical function of the institutions they serve. Briefly put, this involves showing humanity to be naturally divested of an innate access to the divine, in order to grant to the institution a monopoly or near monopoly on the means of grace and salvation. Rather than seeing the institutions they serve as necessarily diverse representatives of unconscious energies seeking to express themselves more fully through religious diversity, institutional theologies either deny this myth-making capacity of humanity or exempt their genesis from it in favor of a purely transcendental and supernatural ancestry.

The benefits of such a theology are immense—for the institution. The tradition such a theology serves can then more easily be presented as guardian of the final revelation, the exhaustive statement of God's intent for humanity, relegating all contending revelations to the status of preliminary divine statements or idolatrous also-rans of purely human origin expressing dubious human values. For Jung such blindness constituted the ultimate contempt for the human soul as the seat from which divinity rises to consciousness:

> The Christian West considers man to be wholly dependent upon the grace of God, or at least upon the Church as the exclusive and divinely sanctioned earthly instrument of man's redemption....
> .... [For the extraverted West] grace comes from elsewhere; at all events from outside. Every other point of view is sheer heresy. Hence it is quite understandable why the human psyche is suffering from undervaluation. Anyone who dares to establish a connection between the psyche and the idea of God is immediately accused of "psychologism" or suspected of morbid "mysticism."[23]

This pathology of an unmitigated transcendentalism Jung frequently describes in terms of uprootedness.[24] The meaning Jung attaches to the term in this context implies that the Western theological—and to a large extent philosophical—traditions have conspired to uproot humanity from its natural access to divinity in its own soul. This process subjects its victims to an acceptance of revealed myths and their symbolic language arbitrarily mediated from above by institutional authority. The hapless believer caught in this schematization of divine-human commerce must struggle to make reasonable sense out of a form of discourse which simply does not submit to a superficial level of reason, which is all such conscious theology has to bring to its interpretation of the myth.

A theological strategy aimed at rerooting or reconnecting the believer with his or her divine ground would have to entail some form of acceptance of Jung's theological anthropology, frankly acknowledging human interiority as the resource from which the deity enters historical consciousness. Were such a view to gain wider acceptance, diverse traditions would feel more at ease in seeing themselves as stones in a yet to be completed divine mosaic, each a partial but needed and valuable expression of the divine intent to become more fully conscious in history. Each could then more gladly look to others for aspects of the potential whole that in their own tradition are absent, and perhaps all could look beyond themselves for a unity transcending their current sum total. Such an attitude, indeed, would make ecumenicism truly possible.

Alas, the humility this requires may be the ultimate heresy to the religious mind possessed of and by its final revelation and committed to what from a broader perspective could be seen as partial. From an historical standpoint, at least, each tradition boasting a final revelation seems destined to take itself literally, seriously and without the humanizing relief available in the recognition of their common origin in the unconscious. And with such intransigence, the more or less innocent victims of this blindness—the legions of disciples and devotees brandishing their different and divisive variations of sacrosanct unintelligibility—seem destined to violently contend with each other and their common humanity, which their faith serves more to remove them from than to acquaint them with.

This split between belief and reason, with the highest value given to the irrationality of faith, is humorously captured in the ditty about the Trinity and its transcendence of human comprehension; where the value of faith is directly proportionate to its unintelligibility, there is every reason for joining in the chorus:

> I wish there were four of 'em,
> So I could love more of 'em.

4

How the West Was Lost

*Our Western intellectualist and rationalistic
attitude has gradually become a sickness causing
disturbances of the psychic equilibrium to an
extent that can hardly be estimated at present.*
— C.G. Jung[25]

Jung's Analysis of Western Spiritual Development

The reduction of statements of faith to the level of sacrosanct
unintelligibility and the blinding of Western consciousness to
the divinity of humanity involved an uprooting or denaturing
not easily or quickly perpetrated. Jung was well aware of this,
hence his diagnosis of the spiritual impoverishment of contemporary Western religious life is not without a keen sense of
the historical developments that contributed to its current bar-
renness.

Jung's reading of history, whether one accepts or rejects it,
is thorough and consistent. To find this dimension of thought
in the works of a man dedicated to the study of the psyche is
rather unexpected but all the more welcome. In fact, Jung's
reflective analysis on how the West so successfully and me-
thodically removed itself from the sources of religious suste-
nance is so nuanced and extensive that it demands a critical
treatment far more thorough than what follows here.

Before looking in detail at Jung's understanding of the
historical development of Western spirituality, certain general
themes in his historical analysis need to be sketched out. In
particular, a general attitude which seems both to rise out of
Jung's reading of history and to control it is based on his
conception of the process known as *enantiodromia*.[26] He bor-

rowed this term from Heraclitus. In Jung's hands the expression takes on a variety of meanings related again to an underlying consistency. It can mean that one extreme will inevitably turn into or elicit its opposite. In this sense Jung uses the term to argue that Christianity's excessive emphasis on a cerebral, if not actually celestial, spirituality led to its historical negation, or at least serious modification in its historical development. This happened as humanity sought to recover those sides of itself which Christianity, due to the historical context that gave birth to it, was obliged to suppress.

But Jung's understanding of enantiodromia does not imply that history, whether societal or personal, is a process of alternating between one extreme and another. Applied to both personal and collective life, it suggests rather that the pendulum swing between extremes tends toward a more humane and inclusive centeredness capable of relating to, even appreciating, extremes without identifying with them.

Jung's position here is of some interest to religious studies because it contains within it a theory of the genesis of revelation itself. In terms of the dynamic described by the concept of enantiodromia, revelation would be what occurs when the collective unconscious proffers a new truth to consciousness, in order to compensate an unhealthy one-sidedness. This can happen in an individual (the popular use of the term "revelation" already implies this), as clearly seen in Paul's conversion on the road to Damascus, or in a society (usually through a powerful religious personality), in the interest of returning that individual or society to its sought-for centeredness and more balanced relatedness. Thus revelations for Jung are not only powerful statements of the unconscious, to be treasured wherever and whenever they appear, they are also vested with an energy that enables or forces those addressed by the revelations to accept them and be changed by them.

In this framework Jung viewed, for instance, the sister revelations of Mithraism and Christianity, which appeared almost at the same time in history. Both revealed the need to restrain libidinal excesses through spiritual suffering and sacrifice; so powerful was the impact of the collective unconscious on collective consciousness that the revelation in its Christian form still provides the West with its major culture hero. Jung writes:

> The meaning of these cults—Christianity and Mithraism—is clear: moral subjugation of the animal instincts. The spread of both these religions betrays something of that feeling of redemption which animated their first adherents, and which we can scarcely appreciate today. We can hardly realize the whirlwinds of brutality and unchained libido that roared through the streets of Imperial Rome.[27]

From this point of view it is possible to discern another reason for Jung's ambivalence toward Christianity as it currently exists. At the beginning Christianity introduced a much needed compensation toward the spirit and away from the unbridled libido which in that ancient society attacked the dignity of so many areas of life. To be effective it had to be itself one-sided. But the demand of the psyche now, according to Jung, is to compensate the one-sidedness of the original Christian compensation.

In this respect Jung argues that Christianity's entrance on the historical scene under the astrological sign of Pisces is noteworthy, for the image of two fishes swimming in opposite directions while bound together through their mouths shows not only the tension of the opposites that Christianity constellated, but also points to Christianity as containing within itself the necessity of its own contradiction.[28] Again, locating this correlation of Christianity and the sign of Pisces in the totality of Jung's thought, the inner contradiction of Christianity would point to a further religious and spiritual consciousness in which the opposites, painfully though needfully constellated by Christianity, may yet be more harmoniously and organically synthesized.

Thus it would be a serious misreading of Jung's thought to imagine that the now needed compensation for Christianity would take the form of an unconscious return to the dehumanizing and ruthless kinds of libidinal activity whose energy

Christianity helped to transform and make usable in the building of Western culture. Rather Jung's attitude is that the necessary compensation would try to hold the gains made in Western consciousness while recovering the price paid for them, namely, the vitalities of the bodily and instinctual side of life, which Christianity tends to hold in contempt. Jung's view, indeed, is that the exclusively conscious and spiritualizing nature of the Christian myth has contributed much to the current illness of both individuals and society.

A question that could well be asked of Jung on this point is one which Paul Tillich raises in a more specifically theological context. Tillich maintains throughout his work that only a symbol can replace a symbol.[29] By this he means that more is involved in the birth of a new symbol or myth than meets the eye. It is Tillich's way of saying that revelations old or new are never solely the product of conscious ego activity. Rather they proceed into consciousness from what he calls the "depth of reason," which he identifies as that point in human being and reason where divinity and humanity intersect. Thus reason cannot author its own mythology.

Jung's thought here is quite compatible with Tillich's. Indeed Jung goes beyond Tillich in providing a much more sophisticated hypothesis of the dynamics involved in the process of a revelatory symbol or myth replacing an incumbent one. Tillich can only state generally that humanity's myth-making function is in the service of its search for "essential humanity," which as a Christian Tillich is forced to identify with the myth of Christ.[30] Jung, however, while respectful of the teleological nature of humanity's search for its essence, would understand this essence to be a unity of opposites, working always toward historical realization through a myth and its attendant consciousness which would be ever more sensitive to this goal. Where Tillich seems compelled to affirm that essential humanity has been definitively depicted in the mythical picture of Christ, Jung's view is that only one of the major opposites, the spiritual, has been championed in the Christ myth—necessarily, in the beginning, in compensation for the excesses of that historical period—and now a counter-myth, one more all-encompassing, is needed as a corrective.

The question provoked here by Jung's thought is this: How and in what direction can the Western spirit look for the revelatory compensation it now needs in the interests of a fuller and safer humanity?

Jung's answer would seem to be that it will ultimately come from the collective unconscious, propelled into consciousness by the suffering attendant upon one-sidedness in interplay with the intent of the unconscious to sponsor, indeed compel, human wholeness. Thus current widespread feelings of uneasiness with, if not outrage at, aspects of the Christian myth may be harbingers of the energies that will ultimately transcend it. Jung's thought further implies, however, that if the new myth is to contain a more humane consciousness transcending what now prevails, it would have to be appreciative of the incumbent myth and incorporate its truth even as it transcended it. Otherwise the resultant enantiodromia would be simply a flight to another extreme as questionably humanizing as the one it replaced.

On a deeper level, it is clear that behind Jung's hope for the development of a more humane and all-inclusive spirituality is his belief that the energies of the Self—the regulating center of the psyche, in charge of the awesome powers of the unconscious—work toward wholeness. If Jung is seriously in error on this point, the even more difficult question arises: "What, then, are the resources humanity has at its disposal for becoming whole?" And if pure consciousness or reason is the only one, then all is lost, for its historical track record in the West since the Enlightenment is as unpromising as that of organized religion.

Another equally important general theme in Jung's reading of Western spiritual development is his contention that Christianity quickly divested itself of any significant relation to human interiority. Its main thrust soon became one of externalism, dogmatic intellectualism or rationalism, and bureaucratic tidiness in the interest of self-preservation. In a critique that is currently gaining some credence in wider scholarship,[31] Jung argues that these moves on the part of institutional Christianity served to remove the mystery of God and Christ from their groundedness in the human psyche, thus making it progressively difficult for the individual to experience them there. In this connection he speaks of the Christian tendency to place God "too much outside," pointing out, sometimes with a note of irony, that the Christian tradition came to place the reality of God almost anywhere but in the soul:

> For this is how Western man, whose soul is evidently "of little worth," speaks and thinks. If much were in his soul he would speak of it with reverence. But since he does not do so we can conclude that there is nothing of value in it. Not that this is necessarily so always and everywhere, but only with people who put nothing into their souls and have "all God outside."[32]

In the face of this quickly institutionalized externalism, argues Jung, the counter and compensating tendencies soon became suspect and then heretical. Thus traditions with a significant emphasis on human interiority came to be fringe traditions in the West. They recurred, but only spasmodically and never with the ability or power to seriously challenge mainstream orthodoxies, which either repressed or ignored them. Among these muted traditions, according to Jung, were the early Gnostics,[33] the mystical tradition,[34] the medieval alchemists,[35] and Platonists of various stripe ranging from Augustine to Kant.[36] Clearly Jung's overview of the Western tradition favors a Platonic over an Aristotelian position, if the characterizing theme of the Platonic tradition is the organic link between the human and that which transcends phenomenal humanity and yet reveals itself through humanity's experience of the link.

Jung concedes that the Aristotelian position has won the West, even as it has uprooted it from its native sense of the divine.[37] He more than once refers to the diminished spiritual perception and sensitivity to the movements of the soul evidenced in the slogan so often adopted by Aristotelian philosophers and theologians: "Nothing in the intellect except through the senses."[38] On this point Jung's critique is virtually identical with Tillich's critique of Thomas Aquinas.[39] By adopting the Aristotelian standpoint, which severs human consciousness from its native awareness of God, argues Tillich, Aquinas made atheism first possible, and then—at least for those sensitive to a spirituality emanating from within—a necessity for the preservation of human dignity.[40] Tillich could thus have counted on Jung's support in the view that the development of Christian theology since the introduction of Aristotle through Aquinas has been one leading consistently to the loss of the inner sense of God.[41]

From the Church Fathers to the Middle Ages

Jung's historical critique of Christianity extends from the patristic period to the major developments in nineteenth- and twentieth-century philosophical and theological thought. Thus Jung appreciates the early fathers such as Justin Martyr for their well-developed sense of the symbolic life and their still free use of symbols drawn from pre- and extra-Christian sources.[42] Yet, as mentioned, Jung feels that Christianity was quickly to emasculate its spirituality by excluding the Gnostics. In Jung's general reading of history, what was rejected in Gnosticism came back in the form of medieval alchemy. This tradition too, from pre-Christian times, sought the transformation of the adept, ostensibly through the physical process of changing base metal into gold, but actually seeking to turn spiritual lead into something more precious (the Philosophers' Stone).

According to Jung, however, by the time the alchemical tradition reappeared in the Middle Ages the human spirit was searching not only for a radical spiritual transformation of soul, it was also seeking to compensate or to complement the spirit of Christ with the more robust and volatile spirit of Mercurius:

> Hesitantly, as in a dream, the introspective brooding of the centuries gradually put together the figure of Mercurius and

created a symbol which, according to all the psychological rules, stands in a compensatory relation to Christ. It is not meant to take his place, nor is it identical with him, for then indeed it could replace him. It owes its existence to the law of compensation, and its object is to throw a bridge across the abyss separating the two psychological worlds by presenting a subtle compensatory counterpoint to the Christ image.[43]

Moving from Jung's evaluation of earlier Christianity toward the present, it is not difficult to understand his appreciation of that side of Augustine's thought which identified in-depth knowledge of oneself with knowledge of God. Jung was also open to the general thrust of Augustine's *Confessions*, in particular the position that the truth of the divine lies in the experience of one's own sacred depths as the goal of the spiritual journey.

This understanding of the spiritual journey as an inner one is also at the heart of Jung's admiration for Bonaventure, who in the thirteenth century followed Augustine in outlining a similar standpoint in his famous *Itinerarium mentis in Deum* (The Mind's Journey to God). From this work Jung was fond of quoting the passage which describes God as a circle whose center is everywhere and whose circumference is nowhere.[44] The obvious implication is that the divine is naturally at the center of every life as the basis of its sense of the transcendent, which the ego can approach but never circumscribe. This too is the meaning Jung attributes to mandala images, whose dynamics point to a regulating center which when approached relates the mind to the totality of which the center is the author.[45]

Occasionally Jung identifies Augustine as an original user of the term "archetype" in a Christian context.[46] Elsewhere he corrects himself and states that the term itself is not to be found in Augustine but only the same idea; in this passage Jung traces the term back to Philo, locating it also in the work of Irenaeus and Dionysius the Areopagite.[47] Here and elsewhere, Jung relates his conception of the archetypes to Plato's understanding of ideas as "universal images that have existed since the remotest times."[48] At the same time, however, he denies borrowing a Platonic world view and forcing it on his psychology, rather than finding its empirical basis in the movements and products of the psyche. Thus he writes, "If I [merely] posited the archetypes, for instance, I would not be a scientist but a Platonist."[49] And in the same vein:

> The old Platonic term differs from the psychological one only in that it was hypostatized [i.e., symbolized in concrete form], whereas our "hypostatization" is simply an empirical statement of fact without any metaphysical coloring.[50]

At times Jung seems to relate the numinosity of the archetypes and their peculiar intensity to the millenarian expectations of the twelfth and thirteenth centuries. For instance, he speaks with a certain sympathetic respect for Joachim di Fiore, the Camaldolese monk and visionary who at the end of the twelfth century thought he discerned the advent of the Age of the Spirit.[51] In one particularly revealing passage (in a letter to his long-time friend Father Victor White), Jung comes close to identifying himself as a modern Joachim who sees the future of the development of consciousness in terms of its progressive assimilation of, and diffusion by, its unconscious ground:

> Thus, making the statement that Christ is not a complete symbol of the self, I cannot make it complete by abolishing it. I must keep it therefore in order to build up the symbol of the perfect contradiction in God by adding this darkness to the *lumen de lumine* [the true light].
>
> Thus I am approaching the end of the Christian aeon and I am to take up Giocchino's [Joachim's] anticipation and Christ's prediction of the coming of the Paraclete. This archetypal drama is at the same time exquisitely psychological and historical. We are actually living in the time of the splitting of the world and of the invalidation of Christ.
>
> But an anticipation of a faraway future is no way out of the actual situation. . . . Christ is still the valid symbol. Only God himself can "invalidate" him through the Paraclete.[52]

Here Jung reveals the eschatological or teleological direction of his thought, which obviously sees the movement of history as one toward a collective consciousness more wholly transparent to its unconscious precedents.

But although Jung discerns powerful archetypal energies at work in the twelfth- and thirteenth-century movements anticipating the third age, or Age of the Spirit, his evaluation of them is highly nuanced and not out of line with contemporary scholarship. In common with other cultural historians, Jung sees in these movements, particularly evident in their longing for a "reformed" Church, the remote causes of the historical sequence which came finally to deny Christianity entirely in the name of reason. Thus the search for a "purer" Christianity, one which would usher in the Age of the Spirit, became instead the initiator of a movement that denied religion in its traditional sense altogether. Such an historical perspective links the longing for more or less minor reforms to the major upheaval represented by the Reformation;[53] this in turn led to the Enlightenment, peaking in the French Revolution, which Jung takes to be the ultimate reversal of Christianity—indeed the Antichrist—crystallized in the form of the Revolution's deification of reason: "The enthronement of the 'Déesse Raison' was, in fact, an anticipation of the antichristian trend that was pursued from then onwards."[54]

In the course of his analysis of these events, Jung's critical response to both the Reform and the Roman tradition is again in evidence. He admires the immediacy of the experience of the "divine fire" and the moral sensitivities made possible by the Reformation, but deplores the loss, culminating in the Enlightenment, of contact with the unconscious and its symbolic expressions, a contact he sees retained, however primitively or unconsciously, in Catholicism.

Indeed, Jung's attitude here is not far from that of Tillich, who called for an "ideal" Christianity combining Catholic substance (contact with the depths of reason and the ground of being) with the Protestant principle (the iconoclastic denial that that through which the ultimate appears can ever be identified with it).[55] In Jung's terms this would mean that an ideal religious—and by implication psychologically healthy—

consciousness would be one in which the ego was nourished by the enlivening energies of the unconscious, without being immersed in them or fixated by one or other of their sometimes dramatic epiphanies in consciousness.

Thus Jung's response to the Enlightenment need not be read as one of total rejection. Rather his attitude is that the gains in consciousness made by the Enlightenment are to be retained but qualified by a reconnection with the unconscious, lest our modern "scientific" consciousness become either sterile or possessed by the very energies—albeit in different form—that the Enlightenment was convinced it had expelled from the human domain with its attack on some of the more repulsive sides of institutional religion.

Jung warns, at times with some vigor, that unless this reconnection with the unconscious takes place, Western humanity could find itself trapped in a truncated consciousness dangerously unaware of the manipulative powers in its own depths. Having freed itself from some of the more obvious repressive features of a previous religion, the West could easily relapse into a far more demonic kind of religiosity, in the form of "isms" and ideologies that invariably move into the void created when reason too smugly thinks it can dismiss the religion-making dimension of the human psyche.

Far better, Jung would argue, to acknowledge and identify the archetypal basis of current socio-economic-political myths —such as Marxism, fascism and capitalism—and so become aware of the true power they have to elicit the faith commitments they do, than to accept them at face value as simply appeals to reason or science. To do the latter is to risk being consumed by a religiosity all the more insidious and inimical to the individual, because the manner in which religious energy functions to engulf the individual is less obvious in these more recent myths than in previous, formally religious, configurations.

Indeed, Jung suggests that the body count left in the wake of the twentieth-century's political faiths equals, if it does not surpass, the carnage left by crusader, inquisitor and the Holy

Wars following the Reformation. One might argue that as medieval man would use such phenomena as change, movement, degrees of perfection and order in the world to point to the existence of God, modern man can point to the human ashes left in the death camps as mute testimony to the ongoing power of faith. Writes Jung: "Not even the medieval epidemics of bubonic plague or smallpox killed as many people as certain differences of opinion in 1914 or certain political 'ideals' in Russia."[56] Jung's challenge to look to the basis of faith in the depths of the human is thus not without social significance. For since it is here that the auto-da-fé, the act of the faith,[57] is born before it proceeds into militant activity in the world, it may be here that its acting out in history can be modified by human consciousness.

Just as Jung works to reveal the archetypal and compelling powers that express themselves through social and political myths, so too he contends that any living philosophy is also an expression of archetypal reality to the extent that it has power over the minds of its adherents.[58] The varieties of philosophical expression could therefore become *ancillae psychologiae,* hand-maidens of psychology, in helping to bring to consciousness the unconscious powers that grip the mind of the philosopher committed to his philosophy.[59] Here the humanizing relativity that characterizes Jung's thought is very much in evidence. Just as the various modern social faiths are valid but partial expressions of humanity's capacities, so also are the currently competing philosophical systems. If they could be seen in this light by their followers, they could perhaps be understood as mutually mitigating and complementary aspects of an unconscious wealth seeking fuller expression than is yet possible through any one particular system.

From this position Jung's thought has within it the norm for differentiating between philosophical and theological standpoints that would be helpful to conscious human development, and those that would be harmful or even entail ultimately the negation of *any* development, through the destruction of humanity itself. The norm would be based on the question of whether or not the patterns of thought in question, be they religious, philosophical or social, lead consciousness beyond itself to the energies within the psyche that work toward its balanced revitalization and empathic extension. With such a norm, patterns of thought that reduce human cognitive and affective resources to those of pure consciousness could clearly be seen as hostile to human life, truncating of its total possibilities and, in our century, leading to forms of collective possession. Such possession is made easier through consciousness' ignorance of the manipulative, unconscious forces (previously called Gods) that play with it all the more freely when consciousness denies their efficacy.

At the other extreme, this norm would also reject those forms of thought which project human capacities wholly beyond the psyche, into divine realities and activities operating in total ontological and epistemological discontinuity with the human psyche. The intrusion of Gods and Goddesses into a psyche divested of their prior presence can only be hostile in their effect, analogous to the injection of foreign material into a living and self-sustaining physical body. With this norm is revealed a core of Jung's thought consistently in opposition to the reduction or devaluation of humanity and its resources to mere mind or consciousness, as implied in systems of unqualified transcendence.

Scholasticism, Mysticism and the Alchemical Tradition

Following Jung's thought on Western development from the High Middle Ages, it is not difficult to understand his abrupt dismissal of Scholasticism as inadequate to the demands of the modern mind and its health, since Scholasticism flourished in a period when the mind was as yet not formally and self-consciously aware of the unconscious.[60] Although Jung is appreciative of the pantheistic elements that enliven the Franciscan tradition (especially in Francis of Assisi and Bonaventure),[61] he challenges modern religious thought to come to terms with depth psychology, just as the medievals came to terms with Plato and Aristotle and incorporated them into their systematic reflections. Thus a modern philosophy that was unaware of the unconscious basis from which living philosophies arise, and a theology unaware of the unconscious origins of the myth on whose behalf it labored, would both be victims of unconscious possession and so unwittingly dedicated to the spread of their own unconsciousness.

Because of his conviction that religious experience in its primordial impact is a direct and powerful experience of the unconscious, and because he believed that this experience was the substance of the mystical tradition, Jung showed a consistent respect for and interest in all forms of so-called mystical expression and experience. Thus his work frequently points to the mystics—such as Meister Eckhart,[62] Jacob Boehme,[63] Angelus Silesius[64] and Nicholas of Flue[65]—as individuals who had experienced directly the power of the unconscious and lived out of the natural religiosity that invariably attaches to such in-depth experience. Were these preferences to be seriously incorporated into theological endeavors, it would mean that a living theology could only arise from the theologian's experience of those powers which Jung locates in the unconscious; such theology, moreover, would be continually enlivened as the theologian sought to give ever more conscious and reflective form to his or her experience.

This would indeed be in marked contrast to the current practice of theology, which too often is an effort to give some form of conscious validation to someone else's experience, itself considered as a piece of conscious though unlikely data. Besides the high rate of burnout such activity fosters in the profession, it augurs poorly for Jung's recommendation that if Christianity is again to come to life and mediate a living truth to wider social circles, it must itself rediscover those sensibilities that derive from an immediate contact with the unconscious.

It was this note of immediacy of experience in the interests of self-transformation that attracted Jung to the alchemical tradition. He came to see it as a medieval anticipation of the transformative experience that modern psychology attributes to the power of the unconscious.

For some time Jung toyed with the idea that Thomas of Aquinas had been the author of the alchemical text, the *Aurora consurgens*. Although Jung found the body of Aquinas's work "not refreshing,"[66] he still entertained the hypothesis that Thomas wrote the work in the brief period after his vision toward the end of his life, just before his death.[67] Jung was later to abandon this hypothesis.[68] It would have entailed too great a transformation of mind and approach for Aquinas to move from the cold and distant logic of the *Summa theologica,* for instance, to the nearly unintelligible emotional intensity characteristic of alchemical writings in general and the *Aurora consurgens* in particular.

But that Jung even played with the idea that Aquinas authored an alchemical work shows Jung's questionable grasp of the Thomistic position on such central issues as the transcendence of God making immediate experience of the divine an impossibility, as is shown in Aquinas's denial of the ontological argument. Indeed, the distance Aquinas placed between the deity and human consciousness is the ultimate antithesis of Jung's contentions that human and divine being intersect in human consciousness, and that no real distinction can be made between the reality of God and the human experience of God. As stated above, this experience is located by Jung in the impact of the unconscious upon the ego. If Jung were truly consistent he would have to indict Aquinas along with Aristotle; both were major influences in removing Western humanity from its psychic origins.

In one of his major works on alchemy, *Mysterium Coniunctionis,* Jung describes the process of alchemical transformation as one of often painful asceticism moving toward a consciousness which, when fully incarnate, evinced a living awareness of its dialectical unity with the ground of all consciousness and being. This is how Jung interpreted the alchemical notion of the *unus mundus.*[69] The mode of thinking which arises from this experience he related to the Western idea of the interpenetration of microcosm and macrocosm.[70] With his concept of synchronicity ("an acausal connecting principle"), Jung takes the position that each time- and space-bound ego has access to the macrocosmic totality through the microcosm in the individual unconscious. This theory, both in alchemy and as formulated by Jung in his writings on synchronicity (which in turn he related to modern physics), presupposes a common ground or collective unconscious from which individual centers of consciousness emerge. This common ground thus makes it possible for individual centers ultimately to be united one with another in patterns of empathic intensity.

Within the spiritual and intellectual atmosphere of his time, Jung came to see himself as a lonely advocate of such a common substratum. He further saw it as possessed of a goal: to realize itself through greater integration with individual centers of consciousness, and so to author patterns of deeper relatedness, both to oneself and to others. Historically this philosophical view disappeared after Leibnitz and Arnold Geulincx.[71] Similarly alchemy was literalized into chemistry; the sought-for unities cherished by its practitioners dissolved into the dissolute facticity and meaninglessness of modern empiricism, while reality was reduced to the merely observable and measurable. Religion also was literalized and, lacking a symbolic understanding of its myths, discredited itself in the battle of the literal-minded that ensued in the dialogue between religion and science.

Kant, Hegel and Modern Theology

Since the unconscious can never be fully depotentiated, especially through so meager a device as conscious denial, Jung can point to certain modern philosophical and theological systems into which the unconscious forced itself, perhaps in spite of the conscious intent of their authors. For instance Jung frequently relates his own standpoint to that of Kant.[72] It is doubtful whether Kant, at least the Kant of the *Critiques,* would appreciate this compliment, if such it be. But the truth of Jung's claim is worthy of discussion, for it may elucidate his suggestion that certain forms of nineteenth-century philosophical thought anticipated the full-blown discovery in the twentieth of that reality modern psychology calls the unconscious:

> It remained for modern science to despiritualize nature through its so-called objective knowledge of matter.... The first beginnings of this [accompanied by a terrific activation of the unconscious] can be seen in Leibnitz and Kant, and then, with mounting intensity, in Schelling, Carus, and von Hartmann, until finally modern psychology discarded the last metaphysical claims of the philosopher-psychologists and restricted the idea of the psyche's existence to the psychological statement, in other words, to its phenomenology.[73]

Jung bases much of the professed similarity between his thought and that of Kant on his conception of the archetypes. Jung understands the archetypes to function in a manner analogous to the structures of the mind that according to Kant control the manner in which we can and do know and behave. Like these Kantian forms and categories, the archetypes are unknowable in themselves. They are known only through their products, such as dreams, symbols, myths and religious experience; hence the existence of these archetypal realities, which according to Jung lie behind and make possible humanity's mythical experience, can be arrived at only through the expressions of that experience in their universal unity and diversity. But, although knowable only through such expressions, these archetypal forces structure humanity's most intense and determinative modes of perception, namely symbol and myth and the ritual which makes the myth more real for those who participate in its re-enactment. Thus both Jung and Kant, claims Jung, presuppose the existence of structuring realities which determine the manner in which we know and act.[74] Moreover, these realities have in some way to be induced from the knowledge and behavior which they engender. For Jung, therefore, the archetypes control our deeper perception and ritual behavior in the same manner as the Kantian categories determine both the possibility and the actuality of our knowledge and moral behavior.

Jung states that the symbol is a phenomenal realization of,

and pointer toward, the noumenon or archetype, which remains unknown in itself and possibly inexhaustible in the variations it can take on in conscious expression.[75] Although Jung occasionally refers to Kant's pre-critical work on psychology,[76] he seems finally to base the substance of his claim to affinity with Kant on the analogy between the archetype as structuring psychic expression and activity and the Kantian theory of structures of knowing and moral behaving.

To the extent that the comparison is valid, it would seem that Jung's understanding of the functioning of the archetype is actually more inclusive of the human totality than is Kant's understanding of the various categories of thought and morality. This is so because in Jung's appreciation of the numinosity or deity-producing quality that can attach to archetypal experience, he includes an affective quality which can command an adherence that functions like the religious experience of faith and likewise demands ritual expression. This note of a more encompassing experience involving affective urgency is absent, or at least muted, in Kant's position, unless a certain numinosity is understood as implicit in the Kantian experience of the moral imperative: "For despite the fall, the injunction that we *ought* to become better men resounds unabatedly in our souls."[77] To identify a numinous experience at the core of Kant's reflection on moral behavior would turn significant components of Kant's thought into a moral or ethical form of the ontological argument (which certain Kantian scholars have in fact done).[78]

Indeed, if a certain numinous experience of the impact of the "ought" on consciousness does lie at the heart of Kant's position on morality, this would align him even closer to Jung; it would mean they both ground their thought on structures that not only precede consciousness but are capable of mediating a sense of divinity or a divine imperative to the ego.

It could also be noted here that Kant was among the first of the significant molders of the modern mind to speak of "archetypal" man.[79] Though Kant's description is limited to a conception of a perfectly moral man, it is not incompatible with Jung's, for it would mean that morality for Kant is in some sense a numinous reality. Jung, in extending the concept of numinosity beyond moral perfection to human wholeness, would in this respect seem to surpass Kant, even as he acknowledges that Kant's explorations of the objective structures underlying human subjectivity preceded his own.

In short, Jung's exploration of human interiority may rightfully be located in continuity with Kant's, but goes beyond Kant's in terms of the wealth that Jung found there, a wealth which could acknowledge the numinous power of moral experience while transcending it toward the higher or broader goal of becoming whole.

Jung's work also contains a number of references to Hegel. Like other historians of philosophy, he understands Hegel as a major respondent to Kant and to the limitations that Kant placed on the mind's capacity legitimately to know God. But Jung's evaluation of Hegel is pervaded with ambivalence. In his major statements on Hegel in the *Collected Works,* Jung describes him as an inflated thinker who responded to Kant's humble acceptance of the limitations of the mind—especially in regard to the mind's presumptions about its knowledge of God—with a grandiose scheme of the absolute and its self-development in history.[80] At times Jung even refers to the pathological implications of Hegel's "impossible language" and his tendency to neologisms. (Heidegger was suspect for the same reasons.)[81]

However, there are currents in Jung's own work that are not so hostile to Hegel. In a letter Jung describes Hegel as a dabbler in psychology, just as he himself was "a philosopher *manqué.*"[82] In the informal medium of correspondence, Jung gives some of the strongest indications that he was fully aware of the profound philosophical and so metaphysical implications in his understanding of the psyche, a side of his thought he tends to disclaim in his published work—perhaps to avoid offending the "scientific" community, as well as the more perceptive among the theologians who might be fearful of the impact of his psychology on their theological understanding of transcendence. Again in one of his later letters Jung admits there may be a greater resonance between his thought and Hegel's than he was aware of, though he continues to deny any direct and conscious influence of Hegel on his thought:

> There is no possibility of inferring a direct dependence, but. . . . there is, of course, a remarkable coincidence between certain tenets of Hegelian philosophy and my findings concerning the collective unconscious.[83]

Indeed, it is true that in the general morphology of their thought both Jung and Hegel perceive the absolute to be engaged in the process of fulfilling itself through conscious conflict in history. Both believe that higher or more inclusive states of consciousness result through conflict being first con-stellated and then resolved (a cornerstone of Jung's psychology and in fact his understanding of the purpose of neurosis). For both, the energies at work in a conflict situation are greater than the seats of either individual or collective consciousness in which the conflict takes place. In this sense both men radically involve the reality of the absolute, immediately and naturally, in the historical unfolding of consciousness, so that what precedes historical consciousness is involved in its completion through historical processes. Both believed that humanity is charged with the historical task of bringing to full consciousness its divine precedent, and in so doing to redeem the contradictions of opposites that exist in this precedent.

The major difference between Jung and Hegel is that Jung emphasizes human interiority as the locus where the divine contradiction is to be experienced and resolved toward more harmonious and inclusive unities, while Hegel locates external historical conflicts as the arena in which the contradiction in the ground of being is incarnated and moved to its resolution. Both thinkers may possess complementary aspects of the same truth. However, in a nuclear age where external attempts at the "resolution" of conflict are potentially so catastrophic, and assuming that the continuation of humanity is a legitimate value, then the Jungian imperative to come to terms with the divine contradiction as it appears in the life and soul of the individual, rather than on the outer battlefield, becomes a major social strategy for collective survival.

In terms of more recent developments in the history of ideas, Jung's consistent preference for those traditions that envisage an organic continuity of the absolute with the fabric of human existence and consciousness is again in evidence. Though he expresses surprise that he could be consciously or unconsciously indebted to nineteenth-century romanticism or idealism,[84] he cites Schelling and some of his contemporaries as anticipating in their speculations the full-blown empirical discovery of the unconscious.[85] And again, though he describes St. Anselm and those drawn to the force of the ontological argument as a type of spirit peculiarly sensitive to the absolute and to the power of universals,[86] it is difficult to deny that Jung's own sensitivities move consistently in that direction. In his own estimate, he considered himself gifted—and sometimes cursed—with a consciousness peculiarly receptive to those powers which grip and transform life, for better or for worse, from a position superordinate to the ego.[87]

That this sense of the immediate presence of Gods and Goddesses controls Jung's reading of the history of thought is again clear in his heated rejection of modern intellectual currents insensitive to the divine proximity. Thus Kierkegaard's efforts to restore a sense of an inorganic transcendence discontinuous with humanity, revealing itself in God's one and final intrusion into history through Christ, are looked upon by Jung as a form of neurosis that inevitably taints the perspective of unqualified transcendentalists. For Jung, Kierkegaard's listening to this unique revelation of God, though admittedly the ultimate weapon against the Hegelian sense of immanence, both deafened Kierkegaard to his own inner dialogue and removed him from life, where the divine is truly encountered:

> That Kierkegaard was a stimulating and pioneering force precisely because of his neurosis is not surprising, since he started out with a conception of God that has a peculiar Protestant bias which he shares with a great many Protestants. To such people his problems and his grizzling are entirely acceptable,

because to them it serves the same purpose as it served him: you can then settle everything in the study and need not do it in life. Out there things are apt to get unpleasant.[88]

Thus "when God appeared to him in the shape of 'Regina,'" writes Jung, "he took to his heels. It was too terrible for him to have to subordinate his autocratism to the love of another person."[89]

For similar reasons Jung is critical of the work of Karl Barth. The concept of a "wholly other" God caused Jung to question how a divinity so foreign to humanity could have a creative relation with it.[90] Like Tillich, and to some extent also Teilhard de Chardin, Jung wonders how a God not intrinsic to the human could address it without destroying it. Thus the thrust of Jung's psychology as it manifests in his perception of history is profoundly supportive of Tillich's panentheism,[91] and of Teilhard's frank call for a Christian pantheism[92] that might restore Christianity to a livelier and more energizing sense of God.

Jung's psychology would therefore seem capable of contributing to a re-evaluation and more critical appreciation of a variety of Christian theological positions and movements. In the light of Jung's critique of the Western tradition, one might well read the Christian neo-theologies of the last 150 years as the rationalization of a timid withdrawal from those modern currents of thought seeking a link between psychology, philosophy and religious experience. At the first Vatican Council (1870), Roman Catholicism responded to these disturbing influences, both philosophical-theological and political, by anathematizing the romantic-idealist philosophical tradition, which the Church rightly perceived to imply a natural intimacy between the divine and the human and so a threat to its own professed role as exclusive mediator of truth and redemption.[93] It declared its leader to be infallible, an embarrassment that nearly a century of well-intentioned mitigation by liberal Catholic theologians has been unable to conceal.[94]

Late nineteenth-century Catholicism also sought refuge in the thirteenth century by imposing on the Catholic philosophical and theological mind the doctrines of Aquinas, a move-

ment that came to be called neo-Thomism.[95] Born under such
forced conditions, neo-Thomism was forced to play surrepti-
tious catch-up ball with Kant, who in his own work denied
many of neo-Thomism's central positions—for instance the
mind's alleged capacity to prove the existence of God.
Whereas Jung's attitude would be that any mind feeling the
need for such proof would already have revealed a peculiar
insensitivity to humanity's natural sense of God, the first Vatican Council decided that this capacity of mind needed formal
affirmation and so was included in its declarations.[96]

Within the modern Reform tradition, Barthian neo-orthodoxy fulfilled much the same role. Perhaps it is a tribute to
this tradition that it did not feel compelled to flee modernity
until after the First World War. But it too anathematized the
romantic-idealist tradition, especially as it was espoused in the
work of Schleiermacher, much admired by Jung, but the bête
noir of the neo-orthodox movement.[97] In place of the Pope,
the neo-orthodox movement infallibilized the biblical Word of
God, and so fled to the sixteenth rather than the thirteenth
century.

In the wake of the personal, intellectual and psycho-spiritual casualties resulting from these strategies of escape in the
name of the preservation of the substance of the tradition,
both neo-Thomism and neo-orthodoxy are largely discredited
today. The human spirit feels justifiably outraged by conceptions of infallibility and claims to exclusive and exhaustive
truth attaching to either book or person—all the more so when
such claims tend to obscure or even to block the experience of
the natural religiosity of the psyche and the attendant healing
and whole-making powers of the unconscious. Much of Jung's
specific genius lay in the manner in which he recalled twentieth-century consciousness to the experience of these realities,
ignored or feared by the religious institutions of his day even
though they owed their own birth and power of renewal to
them.

Looking steadily at the malaise which it had caused in his
clerical relatives and in his patients, Jung as a man concerned
with the human soul was thus forced into more than a passing

familiarity with the historical development of Western spirituality. He was driven to familiarize himself with the pathogenic features of the metaphysical and theological presuppositions that constituted the sickness around him. His reflections seem to coalesce around the conclusion that the Western psyche and soul had lost touch with the healing and native divinity which grounds human life. Historically, those who had pointed to this presence and its power—and in many cases lived out of a direct experience of it—had been shunted to the periphery of respectability. Hence it became Jung's own view as a practicing psychoanalyst that neurosis, especially in the second half of life, is never "cured" without the development or rediscovery of a religious attitude, by which he understands not faith in any particular creed but rather "the attitude peculiar to a consciousness which has been changed by experience of the *numinosum*."[98]

In the final analysis, Jung's reading of history is itself an argument for a re-examination and restoration to stage center of those traditions which point to the natural presence within the psyche of what has ever and always been called God, humanity's ultimate healing and invigorating resource. This could pose some difficulty, because the Church has formally declared many of these streams of thought heretical. But just as in individual life becoming whole can mean facing and consciously integrating those psychic elements which have been excluded or repressed, so also in the life of ecclesiastical or corporate spirituality wholeness may lie in the recovery of "the stone rejected by the builder," rejected in the name of a now sterile and sterilizing orthodoxy.

This is to say that if the shadow whose assimilation could restore fuller life to the Church is to be found in its fringe traditions, such as mysticism both in its orthodox and non-orthodox forms, then it would be only wise for the Church to invest some energy in the re-incorporation of what has been lost by excluding them. In Jung's estimate, at least, such a step could greatly alleviate the illness that we are.

5

Theopathology and Christopathology

In the empirical self light and shadow form a paradoxical unity. In the Christian concept, on the other hand, the archetype is hopelessly split into two irreconcilable halves, leading ultimately to a metaphysical dualism—the final separation of the kingdom of heaven from the fiery world of the damned.

—C.G. Jung[99]

Jung's critiques of the Christian doctrines of God and Christ are too well known to need rehearsal here at length. They must be examined in some detail, however, to show how they illustrate Jung's contention that the Christian myth and its theological elaboration are dangerously incomplete expressions of the totality toward which, according to Jung, humanity's psycho-spiritual life moves. They are also introduced here to show what must happen, in Jung's view, if the consciousness borne by this myth and its attendant theology is to be transcended and their pathogenic potential alleviated.

Note first of all that Jung's attitude toward the Christian doctrines of God and Christ partakes of his general ambivalence toward Christianity. His criticism is coupled with a profound appreciation of their value as expressions of some of the most important movements of psycho-spiritual life. In his major statements on the Trinity, and again in his extended reflections on the Christ figure, Jung demonstrates, true to his methodology, the historical prevalence of Christ-like figures and triadic symbols of deity, in order to show how deeply embedded in the psyche—as the source of religious expression —they both are.[100] Yet combined with this appreciative aware-

51

ness of historical precedent is Jung's allegation that both, though historically of immense value in their Christian variation, stand now in urgent need of being transcended in the service of cultural and psychological wholeness.

Thus in its initial thrust, Jung's essay on the Trinity is most appreciative of the psycho-spiritual truth which that symbol has always sought to convey in its Christian and extra-Christian manifestations.[101] Put succinctly, the substance underlying the variations on the symbol of the Trinity is the process of individuation itself, which lends itself to symbolic expression in triadic form. Symbols of a three-fold deity would then refer to the emergence of the ego (Son, Word) from its source (Father—or Mother-Father, if Gnostic symbolism be allowed), and the synthesis of these polar opposites in the Self (Spirit).[102]

So understood, the symbol of the Trinity would point to the gradual transformation of the individual, as he or she experienced the truth of the Self or Spirit coming into conscious incarnation through the progressive integration of the ego with the centering and expanding energies of the unconscious.[103] As such, the symbol would proceed from, and serve to intensify, the experience of life flowing harmoniously and abundantly between the oppositional poles of ego and unconscious, whose interaction, according to Jung, is the basis of psychic life. Through the symbol of the Trinity, this process is projected into a transcendent life system personified as the Trinitarian God. In this way the symbol functions as a powerful image of how life can move in rhythms of eternal self-renewal, through the interplay of the psychic opposites that constitute the dynamics and structure of all life.

When Jung depicts the same process under the guiding rubric of sacrifice, in his essay on transformation symbolism in the Catholic Mass, the pain intrinsic to the process for anyone who suffers through it is made much more evident.[104] Jung calls the Mass "the *rite of the individuation process.*"[105] In it, through the re-enactment of the central events in the myth of Christ—here understood as a figure representing universal humanity—the ego (Son, Christ) is sacrificed to the unconscious (Father), to rise again in the experience of the Spirit-Self, now not as a distant, unique and isolated event, but rather in the here-and-now consciousness of the participant entering this truth with the help of the rite. In the psychic movement that grounds the Mass (and other rites of renewal), the ego is sacrificed to the unconscious in the interest of resurrection toward a better balanced and more expansive consciousness. The pain in this derives at least partially from the ego's awareness that it is not the master of its own fate. Similarly, the unconscious is sacrificed to the ego, by relinquishing its position of unqualified transcendence and incarnating in finite human life with all the constrictions and suffering this entails.[106]

Thus understood, the atonement worked by Christ and the ritual re-enactment of the truth of Christ would be the "at-one-ment" of the ego with its unconscious energies, manifesting in consciousness as that sense of renewal inevitably generated by the ego coming into closer proximity with its unconscious origins.

For Jung, then, the Mass would not primarily refer to a past event, with magical vicarious benefits for those who somehow participate in its peculiarly unique historical effects. Rather the Mass would be the occasion of the participants' fuller entry into the movements of death and resurrection which with the help of the rite occur in the present. In this sense the Mass is a concrete acting out of a genuinely archetypal pattern. Hence Jung had little respect for theories of vicarious atonement which pointed to some distant event in which the Christ figure, for instance, suffered once and for all time for everyone. Jung's view of Christ's suffering is rather that it symbolizes or exemplifies the suffering that anyone must undergo in the process of maturation. Further, where vicarious atonement is taken literally and historically it could serve to block rather than encourage the maturing process, by alleviating the suffering that can only be lived through by the individual in the process of becoming whole:

In the one case it is merely a question, say, of going to Mass; in the other it is more like Abraham's sacrifice of his son or Christ's decision in Gethsemene. The one may be felt very earnestly and experienced with all piety, but the other is the real thing.[107]

For these reasons Jung can write with great admiration for the psychological meaning and potentially renewing power of Trinity symbols and the rite of the Mass, while his appreciation remains somehow preliminary. His criticism of Trinitarian symbols, for instance, culminates in the suggestion that the Trinity symbol, as well as the experience from which it flows and toward which it leads, needs completion through the integration of all those elements so central to life as experienced by humanity and yet somehow really absent in triadic representations of deity. Here Jung introduces "the problem of the fourth," illustrating that the Trinity finds its natural and, to some extent, demanded completion in a quaternity.[108] Jung even suggests that Trinitarian symbolism actually serves in the too easy dismissal or repression of those elements that are absent from it. The aspects of life most glaringly missing in the Trinity are the material, the feminine and the demonic.

The real absence of the material in the Christian deity points to the whole problem of the meaning of creation in a Trinitarian model of God. In what sense, one may ask, can a life (divine) sufficient unto itself and capable of unlimited self-renewal have any significant commerce with life (human) beyond itself? Or to reverse the question, how can a human life have meaning in itself or for its self-sufficient originating principle?

Jung's general response to this question—one which traditional Christian theology has constantly refused to adopt—is that God needs humanity in order that he may become fully conscious, and especially to become fully conscious of the absolute opposites that exist in the divine creative potential. Thus one of the more important metaphysical implications of Jung's psychology is that human consciousness transcends its divine origin (the unconscious), specifically in its ability to differentiate irreducible opposites and in its capacity to suffer consciously their conflict. In this view, God, as the primal creative source of all latent oppositions, must be understood as that psychic resource in which the opposites remain undifferentiated but far more powerful in their primitive numinosity than can be comfortably contained by the relatively frail capacity of the ego. It is the ego, nevertheless, that remains the historical locus in which the full power and meaning of the divine contradictions are brought to consciousness. This happens, according to Jung's view, through the human suffering that results from becoming aware of and sustaining the undeniable, contradictory truths that are the essence of both the unconscious and the divine.

Such an unconscious God is epitomized for Jung in the arbitrary and capricious Yahweh with whom Job had to contend and ultimately to educate morally, in spite of Job's much more vulnerable standpoint in consciousness:

> Loudly as his [Yahweh's] power resounds through the universe, the basis of its existence is correspondingly slender, for it needs conscious reflection in order to exist in reality. Existence is only real when it is conscious to somebody. That is why the Creator needs conscious man even though, from sheer unconsciousness, he would like to prevent him from becoming conscious.[109]

Yahweh's state of consciousness is characterized by Jung as that of someone unconsciously possessed by the opposites and so whipped back and forth by their power. In Yahweh's case this showed itself in the contradiction involved in divine claims to be the seat of truth, justice and power, by a deity so susceptible to the demonic as to allow a just man to be arbitrarily set upon by Satan. Jung identifies Job's awareness of the divine self-contradiction as the ego's awareness of the profound opposites it is faced with in its own depths. And yet this awareness, though painful in itself, is the first step to the conscious differentiation of opposites in the interest of their eventual unification. In this sense, Jung implies that Job's confrontation of Yahweh with his self-contradictions and infantile tendency to swing between the opposites actually shamed Yahweh into becoming fully incarnate in the Christ figure—surely the most creative interpretation yet for the divine motivation behind the historical appearance of Christ:

> To sum up: the immediate cause of the Incarnation lies in Job's elevation, and its purpose is the differentiation of Yahweh's consciousness. For this a situation of extreme gravity was needed, a *peripeteia* charged with affect, without which no higher level of consciousness can be reached.[110]

With the Incarnation, then, the absolute contradictions in the ground of being were historicized in a no less absolute contradiction that would demand their eventual embrace.

When Jung's psychology is taken as an organic whole, it can be seen—and this becomes particularly evident in his work on Job—that Jung is proposing a counter-myth to myths of unmitigated divine transcendence. Such myths center on an omniscient and omnipotent, self-sufficient God who arbitrarily creates and, in the face of an initial human failure, arbitrarily intervenes in His redemptive initiative. Jung's counter-myth reverses this, having humanity with its differentiating consciousness inextricably engaged in the historical redemption of an unconscious but extremely powerful God. In this God are present all the conflicting absolutes which have torn asunder personal lives and bloodied the course of history. These absolutes in their naked power can take possession of consciousness and bind it in undying fidelity to one or the other extreme, or bat the ego back and forth between conflicting opposites much as a tennis ball moves between opposing players.

The suffering of humanity in the redemption of God would thus entail bringing to conscious life, and to some form of synthetic harmony, the many powerful opposites that live in the divine ground of historical consciousness. For Jung, the pain of suffering these contradictions consciously is the point at which divine and human suffering coincide. This point of coincidence is also the substance of Yahweh's answer to Job as Jung interprets it. The answer is that God must suffer through humanity, in the interest of their mutual completion. This is Jung's reading of the purpose of the Incarnation:

> There is no evidence that Christ ever wondered about himself, or that he ever confronted himself. To this rule there is only one significant exception—the despairing cry from the cross: "My God, my God, why hast thou forsaken me?" Here his human nature attains divinity; at that moment God experiences what it means to be a mortal man and drinks to the dregs what he made his faithful servant Job suffer. Here is given the answer to Job, and, clearly, this supreme moment is as divine as it is human, as "eschatological" as it is "psychological."[111]

The immense hope that Jung holds out to humanity is that its *conscious* suffering of the divine opposites will arrest the blind movement of mankind toward self-destruction. His psychology, again when taken in its totality, further holds out the hope that humanity's patient suffering of the opposites is in some way actually sponsored by the divine (God, the Self), which seeks self-realization on both personal and societal levels. This would mean that the conscious suffering of the divine self-contradictions is in the service of the emergence of higher unities of consciousness capable of embracing a wider and more variegated humanity. Such an encompassing compassion is for Jung the natural goal of the suffering itself. God and humanity have first to become fully aware of their contradictory natures before they can move toward a synthesis of their opposites.

The psychological drive to the realization of these potential unities, and the experience of grace which follows to the extent these unities are realized, constitute for Jung the ineradicable basis in the human spirit for the so-called third age, the Age of the Spirit. This drive is the substance of the millenarian expectation engrained in humanity's psyche and spirit. As such, it is the ultimate mover and goal of history. For Jung, however—and this is where his thought is jarring for the mass-minded devotee of the social solution—it is a collective goal which can be realized only through the individual consciously suffering the power of the opposites as they are experienced in the depths of one's personal spiritual life. Only through the individual's lonely wrestling with the divine contradiction as it manifests in his or her own life can God, the individual and history be redeemed.

From this point of view, the greatest contribution the individual can make to the realization of history, and indeed the very survival of mankind, is the conscious grappling, on a daily basis and in the context of active social life, with the deities and demons that tyrannically contend for a one-sided grasp of his or her consciousness—the psychological precedent to the imposition of external tyranny.

At this point it becomes rather obvious that in Jung's psychology the metaphysic of the Self is the ultimate basis for hope. For when all is said and done, his thought seems consistently to imply that the Self, as regulating center of the psyche, will resolve the contradictions it both contains and sponsors in historical conflict. The final goal, then, for both the individual and for mankind, would be patterns of incredibly wealthy harmonies. And the basis of this, the unitive powers of the Self, Jung locates not beyond but within the individual psyche.

The second real absence in the Christian Trinity is that of the feminine.[112] Here Jung's critique of the Trinity symbol flows naturally into his Christological reservations. The Christ figure is male and his relations with the feminine remain ambiguous. There is no evidence within the canonical version of the myth that he was able to commit himself to a woman, though there appears to have been a number in his entourage. This absence of a significant feminine presence both in Christ's life and in the Trinity is no doubt a major contributor to Christian misogyny, so much a concern of contemporary scholarship.[113] Jung proposes, however, that this deficiency has been alleviated, at least within the Catholic community, by the restoration of the Goddess in the figure of Mary. Indeed, he considers nineteenth- and twentieth-century Catholic Marian dogmatic declarations, especially that of the bodily Assumption of Mary into heaven (1950), to be among the most significant religious events in the West since the Reformation.

Jung's appreciation of Catholic Marian doctrinal declarations remains unqualified by the fact that both were accompanied by two of the most repressive declarations in recent papal history. The definition of the Immaculate Conception in Pius IX's reign in 1854 was followed in the reign of the same Pope ten years later by the infamous Syllabus of Errors condemning the liberal and liberating movements of thought in the nineteenth century.[114] Similarly, the doctrine of the Assumption, declared in Pius XII's reign on November 1, 1950, was preceded on August 12 of that year by the encyclical *Humani Generis,* which once again condemned the liberal movements in the Church that had surfaced since the war and ultimately were to break through again in Vatican II.[115]

An historian might wonder why the Roman turn to the Goddess seems to have been so closely associated with the repression of other liberating movements within Catholicism. Whatever the answer to this psycho-historical question, Jung saw the Marian revival in Catholicism as the necessary antidote for the loss of the symbolic sense within the Reformed Church as it moved to embrace historical rationalism and literalism—a tendency which Jung understands to have reached a certain culmination in Rudolf Bultmann's program of demythologization. ("But what can one expect in an age when the official spokesmen of Christianity publicly announce their inability to understand the foundation of religious experience!")[116] Jung's strong feelings on this point are evident in his letters, where he declares the Catholic revivification of the Goddess in the form of Mary to be a "momentous step," revealing to all that Protestantism is "way behindhand in the matter of dogmatic development."[117] And to Father Victor White Jung candidly states his view of the Assumption in these terms:

> It is more than probable that the idea of the Assumptio did not begin its real life in apostolic times but considerably later. The miracle of the Assumptio obviously began to operate noticea-

bly from the VI century onwards only. If the A. means anything, it means a spiritual fact which can be formulated as the
integration of the female principle into the Christian conception of the Godhead. This is certainly the most important
religious development for 400 years.[118]

Jung's interpretation of the psycho-spiritual genesis of
Catholic Marian doctrine, though it may seem outrageous to
orthodox ears, is worthy of some comment. First it should be
pointed out that it has no basis whatever in the consciousness
of mainstream Catholic theology, which spares no effort, theologically and devotionally, in denying divinity to Mary and
reserving it exclusively for Christ. But this conscious denial of
Mary's divinity makes Jung's remarks all the more interesting.
He might be read to imply that precisely because Christianity
has reserved deity to the masculine, the divinization of Mary—
though consciously denied by the preservers of orthodoxy who
did it—may have become an unconscious historical necessity.
Thus the process initiated by the Council of Ephesus in 431
(which first restored the Mother Goddess to a flagging Christianity) was completed in 1950 with Mary's elevation to heaven,
where her presence complements the austerity of the all-male
Trinity. For Jung, the missing feminine, in the person of
Mary, would therefore reclaim its rightful place in the realm
of the divine, and at least one branch of Christianity could
proclaim the *hieros gamos,* the sacred wedding between God
and Goddess that renews the earth and life at all levels.

However, the introduction of a sexual image, even if mari-
tal, throws into even higher relief the problem of the Catholic
Goddess. For only her immaculate aspect is divinized, and
that by only a part of the total Christian community. Those
sides of the feminine personified in such non-Christian figures
as Circe, Venus, Artemis, Hecate and Kali are excluded from
the heaven in which the Virgin-Mother rules. Thus the image
of Mary divinizes the virginal and the maternal, while processes of movement from one state to the other are banished
from heavenly realms, hidden even from the eyes of an omniscient God.[119]

No doubt it is better to have a pantheon populated by one Goddess than none at all, but the Christian image of the Virgin-Mother in her one-sided stainlessness excludes important elements of humanity and thus contributes to, rather than relieves, Christian misogyny. Jung himself was well aware, perhaps before his time, that the Christian hostility to the feminine, as a threat to male, spiritual perfection, lay behind the barbarism and brutality of the witch-hunters and inquisitors.[120] A humanly unreal virgin and mother, when taken literally and not as a symbol of spiritual self-renewal or self-birth—as Jung would interpret all symbols of parthenogenesis—can only contribute to hostility toward real women, and confirm the threat that women presumably pose to a masculine spirit in pursuit of a perfection defined in terms that virtually exclude a living relation to the feminine.

From a Jungian perspective, this form of unrelatedness in masculine spirituality destroys not only the feminine (and those women subjected to it), it also destroys the male spirit possessed by it. For if one grants to Jung the foundational premise of his psychology—that psychic maturation, and so spiritual maturity too, can only take place through a relationship to the contrasexual energies both in the individual psyche and in other humans—then it becomes difficult to deny the link his thought establishes between pathology and the pursuit of a perfection based upon the exclusion of the feminine (or the masculine), whether within or beyond the individual soul. Such a conception of perfection would be, needless to say, pathogenic for either sex.

Christianity's recovery of a fuller relationship to the feminine would thus require, in the logic of Jung's own thought, the introduction into the Christian pantheon of Goddesses whose presence there might make its current occupants decidedly uneasy. To really face the implications of Jung's concept of wholeness would be to force the Christian mind to ask if those missing Goddesses can be admitted without the loss of its identity, or if they can any longer be denied admission without the loss of its health. This question might go deeper than the perhaps too-easy appeals occasionally made by Jungians to the Black Madonna and to Magdalene figures as somehow the compensating shadow for the one-sided Immaculate Goddess. For it would imply that if Christianity is truly to be the vehicle of the epiphany of a wider and more humanizing range of feminine divinity, then it may legitimately be called upon to transcend itself in such a manner as to risk self-loss.

The final real absence in the symbol of the Trinity is that of evil. Jung's views on this matter appear most forcefully in his long and eventually acerbic correspondence with Father Victor White on the Christian conception of evil as a *privatio boni,* a privation or absence of good.[121] Jung's general position in this prolonged debate was that good and evil are equally real, at least as they manifest in the psyche (which for Jung is the only place that any kind of reality can and does manifest). Thus Jung opposed what he took to be an evasive trivialization of evil implicit in its definition as simply the absence of good.[122]

But in and through this issue one can see the general thrust of Jung's psychology in both its structure and dynamics. One can also see why he considers the absence of evil in the triadic symbol of the Godhead, and its absolute rejection by the Christ figure, as standing in need of eventual correction. Indeed, in this area of Jung's thought his critique of the Trinity and of the Christ figure tend to coincide. Rather than imagining the Trinity as self-sufficient, wholly conscious and unequivocally good, Jung proposes a counter-image. The Godhead as ultimately the generative source of everything would contain all the undifferentiated opposites, including those of good and evil. In the unfolding of this matrix in and through historical consciousness, the opposites in the unconscious God are gradually differentiated. At the stage of developing human and religious consciousness—represented in the Christian myth by the Christ figure's absolute rejection of evil, personified in the figure of Satan—historical consciousness breaks through to the realization that the ground of consciousness and of being is involved in a contradiction, one that has to be made fully though painfully conscious in history if it is eventually to be resolved there.[123]

In Jung's counter-myth, the Father would be the generator of Christ and Satan, his light and dark sons, whose opposition the Christian myth brings to full historical consciousness. But this state of absolute differentiation and enmity, though of inestimable value—and in Jung's opinion one of the major contributions made to religious consciousness by Christianity— is merely a penultimate stage, a preliminary differentiation and enmity preparatory to a fuller synthesis:

> In our diagram [below], Christ and the devil appear as equal and opposite, thus conforming to the idea of the "adversary." This opposition means conflict to the last, and it is the task of humanity to endure this conflict until the time or turning-point is reached where good and evil begin to relativize themselves, to doubt themselves, and the cry is raised for a morality "beyond good and evil." In the age of Christianity and in the domain of trinitarian thinking such an idea is simply out of the question.... [but] the unspeakable conflict posited by duality resolves itself in a fourth principle, which restores the unity of the first [Father] in its full development [Spirit]. The rhythm is built up in three steps, but the resultant symbol is a quaternity.[124]

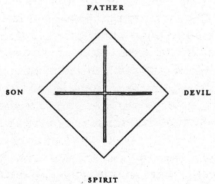

To look upon the mutual antagonism of Christ and Satan as final and irreconcilable, the basis for an eternal separation of sheep from goats, would in Jung's terms be an admission that the conflict of opposites within the Godhead, when made historically evident, defied human solution and so would proceed into eternity in the forms of those committed to heaven and to hell. Ultimately this would also mean that humanity was unable significantly to help, let alone redeem, the divinity in the resolution of the absolute conflicts that characterize its life.

Thus the logic of Jung's position would demand in both personal and historical life the reunion, or at least the guarded cooperation, of Christ and Satan, as psychological consciousness approached the Age of the Spirit, whose specific feature would be the unity of the divine oppositions—generally deemed a priori creative, but heretofore realized in history predominantly in configurations of hostility. In this sense the embrace, so to speak, of Christ and Satan would be one of the major syntheses demanded by Jung's eschatology.[125]

The degree of difficulty in bringing about such a rapprochement illuminates the manner in which Jung would conceive of truly creative and redemptive suffering in the processes of historical at-one-ment ushering in the psychological eschaton or goal. For if humanity is to move toward the resolution of the absolute contradictions in personal and collective life, Jung would invite the individual caught up in these opposites to participate in the suffering depicted in the image of the Christ figure dying in the agony of suspension between yes and no.[126] Only the pain of bearing this contradiction can lead to that resurrected consciousness "beyond good and evil," where divine and demonic recognize their common origins, their implacable historical hatred and, hopefully, their deeper compulsion to unite again beyond enmity.

Significantly, in a late and very candid letter to Father White, Jung writes that although he may consider himself a modern Joachim of Fiora,[127] somewhat ahead of his time with a vision of a new consciousness, the truth of Christianity can only be transcended if it be lived through:

> It would be a lack of responsibility and a rather autoerotic attitude if we were to deprive our fellow beings of [the Christian symbol] before they had a reasonable chance to under-

stand it thoroughly, and all this because it is not complete if envisaged from an anticipated stage we ourselves in our individual lives have not yet made real.[128]

By this Jung not only concedes at least a partial value to Christianity, he also clearly infers that only through the individual's bearing of the divine contradiction in his or her own spiritual life can a higher or more harmonious stage of historical consciousness emerge. In this sense, the agony of human spirit and consciousness becomes the arena where the divine ground of that consciousness suffers the conflict of its own opposites in the interests of completing itself. The human suffering so intimately and necessarily involved in the transformation of the divine is the price to be paid for the peace and blessedness of the coming Age of the Spirit.

The split between the absolutes of good and evil is not the only split constellated by the Christian myth and now asking for historical healing. Jung felt that the Christ figure splits not only good and evil but also spirit and full-blooded bodiliness.[129] Jung argues that the one-sided spiritual emphasis that was initially so valuable a component of the Christian compensation stands now itself in need of compensation, through a fuller acceptance of the bodily, the instinctual and the sexual, all muted elements in the received figure of Christ. As already indicated, Jung did not counsel a regression to the unrestrained libidinal expressions that characterized the age into which Christianity came; he simply pointed to a recovery of those realities that Christianity may have been forced to demonize in order to control. In this now historically necessary synthesis of body and spirit, Christian values would be respected even as they were transformed by the acceptance of what had previously been excluded.

Jung's thought does not take kindly to exorcisms. Rather it moves by its very nature to higher syntheses, assimilation as opposed to exorcism, arguing that more all-embracing configurations of humanity and its consciousness are demanded by the unconscious, the source of life, in order to be realized *in* life.

The radical nature of the re-unification of body and spirit

with which Jung challenges Christian spirituality is forcefully illustrated in a tale he borrows from the Gnostics. In a simpler, if not infantile, Christian piety, stories are told of the baby or child Jesus exercising his divine prerogative by turning clay models of birds and other creatures into living beings. In the Gnostic version, a more adult Jesus, accompanied by a woman Mary, goes to a mountain top (the archetypal location for many a transfiguring event). There the Christ figure again exercises his divine prerogative, this time producing from his side a full-grown woman with whom he proceeds to make love before Mary's shocked eyes. He then told Mary, " . . . quod oporteat sic facere, ut vivamus" (that this was to be done that we may have life).[130]

This apocryphal tale as used by Jung makes two telling points. Firstly, sexual activity and imagery is attached to Jesus and associated with life, not death as is too often the case in traditional Christian thought. Secondly, and of more importance, Jung's interpretation of this theandric event goes far beyond a literal, probably lecherous and certainly infantile view of a divine figure creating a submissive physical lover. Rather Jung's understanding sees Jesus performing a life-giving act open to all. Jesus here has intercourse with his anima in giving birth to the Self.

Thus the universalization of the demand to imitate Jesus, to do this and live, is not a challenge to match his miraculous powers in the production of a lover. Rather it is a challenge to experience the ever present and ever possible love affair with one's own psychic sexual counterpart, in bringing to birth a consciousness of the Self more intensely enlivened with the energies of the unconscious. In this sense the love affair never ends nor does it falter with age.[131]

In more orthodox Christian usage, a variant of the words in the story, "Do this and you shall live," often accompanies the giving of a religious rule book to someone being initiated into an intensified form of Christian life through membership in a religious community. This commonly involves taking vows toward perfection, and one of the vows is usually chastity, understood as sexual abstinence. If this vow is taken in the context of a spirituality or a theological anthropology that remains unaware of, and so excludes, the possibility of inter-course with the psychic contrasexual, we may wonder at the quality of life being proferred to the initiate. From a Jungian perspective, the words might better be, "Do this and you shall die." For in Jung's thought it is only through the ego's relation to the contrasexual in the unconscious—the anima in a man, the animus in a woman—that the life-renewing energies of the unconscious enter conscious life. A person cut off from a living and life-giving relationship with an external man or woman, and also cut off from the more intense relationship with the psychic powers which give rise to these external relations, has no choice but depression and the varieties of spiritual death that invariably follow. One is here reminded of Christ's words, "What doth it profit a man to gain the world and lose his soul [anima]?" To which the Gnostic Christ would readily reply, "Nothing at all."

The point is that a Christianity which may have rightly needed to restrain the sexual excesses of the society in which it first appeared, and indeed excesses in any historical period, may have come to see sexuality itself as somehow peripheral to life, and so conceived of the possibility of healthy life, even or especially the life of spiritual perfection, without it. In some external and merely physical sense the sexual dimension of life could perhaps be considered peripheral, and so dispensa-ble for a "higher" goal, though this is a dubious proposition at best. But in the light of Jung's exploration of human interior-ity, the reality of sexuality is neither dispensable nor peri-pheral to the life of the soul and to spiritual maturation. For Jung, individuation cannot take place without an intense rela-tionship to the contrasexual. Thus the question is not *whether* the sexual will be faced in the pursuit of spiritual and human growth, but *where*. If it is sacrificed in its external manifesta-tions, this can be healthy only if the sacrifice intensifies the inner relationship. Otherwise such spiritual heroics, though they may win a "supernatural" crown, can only make natural humans sick.

Looking to the orthodox expressions of Christian spirituality for resources upon which to build the now urgently needed spiritual synthesis of body and soul, one finds little help except in the imagery of certain mystics. Sexual images of unity with God are sparse. There is the traditional image of the Christian as the bride of Christ. Mechthilde of Magdeburg speaks with a refreshing frankness of her courtly love with a youthful Christ figure.[132] Julian of Norwich speaks of the maternal side of Christ,[133] and Jung himself refers to the androgynous nature of the Christ figure.[134] In his mystical Christology, Jacob Boehme has references to the "kiss of Sophia," Sophia being the feminine counterpart of the Logos principle.[135]

The writings of mystics may be helpful in that they at least introduce sexual imagery into the relation between the masculine and the Christ figure. Yet their value is rendered somewhat ambiguous by the homosexual connotations that might attach to some of the images, especially in the literal-minded. The truth is that mystical writing, although it usually derives from an intense experiential familiarity with the inner life, is readily dismissed by prevailing Western religious preferences, which are far more rational and hard-minded. To take the mystic seriously would involve a new-found respect for the unconscious as the breeder of religious experience. For the reasons given above, this remains a threat to the transcendentalist position still in control of the Western religious mind.

For the majority, then—that is, for the non-mystical Christian—Jung's diagnosis of Western spirituality as pathological still holds. Its pathological nature for Jung always comes to a focus in its splitting one-sidedness, that is, in its emphasis on only one side of the human and humanizing truth: the unqualified goodness and light of the Trinitarian God and its full historical incarnation in the Christ figure, born of a stainless woman without male cooperation. All other aspects of life are muted, excluded or rendered positively demonic by the myth. Hence these other aspects, according to Jung, now clamor for re-admission into a more total view of the human, toward which humanity is inexorably driven by the psycho-spiritual forces which give rise to both its consciousness and its conscious aspirations.

Cooperating with transpersonal forces that move individual and society in the direction of wholeness is always painful, because in one way or another it demands acknowledgment of our partialness and the abandonment of the cherished idols of our incompleteness. In this sense the vice of idolatry as the worshipping of developmental truncatedness is for Jung the ultimate sin against the Spirit, whose nature is to move toward ever more encompassing configurations of totality. For many, the rewards of clinging to spiritual infancy in the name of fidelity or commitment to a final revelation are too great to be abandoned. The security of certitude, of possessing the final truth as a member of the chosen people, a people set apart, simply outweighs the pain of disorientation that invariably accompanies the risk of growth.

And so, both for those who cling to the conventional Christian revelation in the name of a dubious faith and for those who are compelled by the surge of inner and outer forces to transcend it, Jung's thought remains a challenge to the Christian mind to reflect at length on the illness that we are.

Jung's mandala, "Window on Eternity"

6

The Final Option:
Mandalic versus Holocaustic Faith

*The afternoon of humanity, in a distant future,
may yet evolve a different ideal. In time, even
conquest will cease to be a dream.*
—C.G. Jung[136]

Jung's critique of Christianity implies a certain teleological understanding of the movements of energy in both the personal and the collective psyche. In reality these movements are inseparable and ultimately one. Both are energized by the basic impulse of the psyche toward wholeness. At the individual level this movement is the essence of what Jung calls the process of individuation. On the collective level, taken as the goal of history, it becomes the basis of Jung's implicit eschatology.

Since the two movements are in effect one, for Jung the greatest contribution an individual can make to the realization of history is to attempt to realize the Self in his or her own life. Similarly, the degree of realization of the Self in any individual life always combines a personal and a universal or eschatological element. In Jung's myth of history, especially as set out in his visionary *Septem Sermones ad Mortuos* (Seven Sermons to the Dead), the dead return to ask the living to solve the problems of historical life.[137] Contrary to certain understandings of the Christian myth, the dead possess no greater knowledge of truth from their position beyond life and historical consciousness. Thus Jung's allegedly playful version of Gnostic insight implies that the goal of history is to be realized within history, through the transformation of con-

71

sciousness as it progressively assimilates more and more of its unconscious origins. No discrete power, therefore, could helpfully intervene in the culmination of history, or even significantly illuminate it with revealed truths, without the cooperation of human consciousness with this power as it worked to consciousness from its position within the psyche yet transcendent to the ego.

In simpler religious language, this would entail the movement of history toward that state of consciousness, individual and collective, which is captured in such images as the beatific vision, heaven, the kingdom of God, eternal life and so on. It would describe a condition in which individual centers of consciousness are peculiarly transparent to, and expressive of, their common ground and creative and enlivening origin. But for Jung, the substance of these images only becomes real in historical consciousness to the extent that they are experienced in individual centers of consciousness in such a way as to alter history on a collective level.

Here again one encounters Jung's insistence that only the individual is the bearer of meaning and so the maker of history. From this it follows that historical change is to be worked through the transformation of individuals who consciously cooperate with the whole-making energies of the unconscious, as the source of consciousness and so of history. Transformation imposed by a deity external to history would both offend the natural movement of historical consciousness and truncate the wholeness to which Jung sees both individual and collective life called. Again, the ultimate sin against the Spirit would be a premature foreclosure on history's intended or potential harmony, by a too early or too one-sided revelation taken as final but tending in fact to be terminal.

At the heart of much of Jung's uneasiness with contemporary Christianity lies the conviction that it no longer serves the emerging unities and harmonies toward which personal and historical development move. Although he concedes its contribution to the development of Western civilization, he sees it currently as opposing the deepest energies of the psyche, which "want" to move individual and history into patterns of personal integration and extended sympathy and relatedness. In this sense, then, Christianity impedes, rather than contributes to, the historical and psychological development of mankind—if we accept the contention at the basis of Jung's psychology, namely that becoming whole is the ultimate value and goal of the history-making psyche.

In the previous chapter were sketched in summary fashion the three major absences in the Christian myth, particularly evident in the dogma of the Trinity: the realities of matter, woman and evil. Though Jung understands these lacunae to have been necessitated by the demands made on the myth by the society it then had to address, yet in the present historical situation, he argues, these absences deprive the devotees of the myth of access to the fullness that the psyche both demands and makes possible.

But there is a second critical theme running through Jung's work, one which addresses not only the specific partialities of the Christian myth but the pathogenic features of monotheistic-transcendent myths in general. Here Jung's critique extends beyond Christianity to embrace all of the major monotheisms. This is so because the spirit of Jung's thought, based on his understanding that the psyche's energies naturally move toward totality, demands that any religion claiming to have a monopoly on a final exhaustive revelation must eventually come to some saving doubt and humanizing relativization of such a claim. Jung further implies that they could be helped in this humbling process by their recognition, if they could ever make it, of their common origins in the collective unconscious of mankind.

Jung implies in certain of his statements that this might be an easier task for the Eastern religions than for those in the West, since at least some streams of Eastern thought are familiar with the natural divinity of the individual, and so with the proposition that the discovery and experience of God and of the individual center or Self are ultimately identical.[138] However, for the majority of the followers of Yahweh and for

those devoted to the Christian divine triad originating with the
Father God, as well as for those faithful to Allah, such a
radical conception of divine immanence remains, in the main,
heretical. It is this unqualified sense of divine transcendence,
so easily leading to claims of exclusive revelation, that lies
behind Jung's complaint that the Christian tradition has emp-
tied the soul of a native divine presence and put "all God
outside":

> Whoever speaks of the reality of the soul or psyche is accused
> of "psychologism." Psychology is spoken of as if it were "only"
> psychology and nothing else. The notion that there can be
> psychic factors which correspond to divine figures is regarded
> as a devaluation of the latter. It smacks of blasphemy to think
> that a religious experience is a psychic process. . . .
>
>   Faced with this situation, we must really ask: How do we
> know so much about the psyche that we can say "only" psy-
> chic? For this is how Western man, whose soul is evidently "of
> little worth," speaks and thinks. If much were in his soul he
> would speak of it with reverence. But since he does not do so
> we can only conclude that there is nothing of value in it. Not
> that this is necessarily so always and everywhere, but only with
> people who put nothing into their souls and have "all God
> outside."[139]

When the one true God is "all outside," he can then sponsor from a position of discontinuous transcendence the absolute revelations that pit one community of believers against
the others. Given the immense possessive power that attaches
to faith—since it derives its energies from the awesome might
of the archetypal world—it is no wonder that blood baths have
been the historical result in the West from the three sets of
distinct and competing revelations from the three "one and
only" Gods. When three Gods author three revelations, the
historical imperative, at least to date, has been "convert or
kill."

The survival of mankind can no longer depend on this kind
of competition, if indeed it ever could. The holocaustic potential of such blind and absolute faith is now self-evident, as is
Jung's timely warning that the religious energies that sponsor

explicitly religious genocide are not eliminated with a rational critique of religion (such as the Enlightenment offered to the West). Rather the religion-making energies in the psyche are channeled instead into declarations of political faith; there they continue their bloody progress through history, as witness the numerous twentieth-century holocausts in an age of professed non-belief.

When these implications of Jung's psychology are squarely faced, the questions inevitably arise: "What protection does humanity have then from the Gods? How can it avoid the faith that kills?"

Jung offers no easy answers. The realization that the Gods and Goddesses dwell in the human psyche, from where they sally forth to possess individual and community, does not in itself limit their capacity to either wreak havoc or confer grace.[140] On the contrary, Jung warns humanity that it cannot divest itself of its God-making tendencies any more than it can cease to breathe, grow hair or write poetry. Indeed, from a Jungian perspective one could argue that if the Enlightenment through its critique of religious dogma had succeeded in eliminating the religious instinct,[141] this would have been its crowning glory. If sustained and significant atheism were a human possibility, then human dignity would demand it. According to Jung, humanity does not have a Godless option. The energies that express themselves in religious symbol, creed and rite, when discredited in any particular form simply reappear in some other equally absolute and potentially destructive "ism."

By identifying the unconscious as the source of every God or Goddess who ever, in whatever guise, addressed mankind, Jung challenges humanity to take heed of this side of itself, to gain a heightened awareness of the direction from which it is approached by the deities and to enhance its appreciation of their continued power. Put briefly, Jung is saying that since mankind cannot divest itself of its relation to Gods and Goddesses, it would therefore be in its best interests to face that side of itself from which they come, in the hope of teasing from them a myth which would be safer for its collective survival and enrichment.

It is in this area—his reflections on the psychic well-springs of human religiosity—that Jung's work may eventually be recognized as having profound implications for the survival of humanity. For Jung demands of humanity the admission that it is religious to and in its core. He accompanies this demand with the caution that unless mankind comes to terms with this intensely divisive, and often murderous, side of itself, then it is likely that the logic of transcendence will be acted out globally in a final solution, demanded by the final revelation(s).

Fortunately, there is in Jung's thought the outlines of an answer to the problems posed by his psychology, in regard to the potentially destructive consequences of militant monotheisms. For his analysis of the psyche claims to find endemic to it a deeply rooted possibility of a faith experience that would counter the holocaustic inevitability of discrete and wholly transcendent Gods authoring mutually contradictory revelations.

Jung's alternative model could be called mandalic faith. It would be based on the experience of psychic energies as they are symbolically expressed in the form of a mandala (a Sanskrit word meaning "circle"), which Jung calls "the psychological expression of the totality of the Self."[142] Jung understands mandala images to be essentially religious, pointing to the presence of God or the Self at the center of every human being, the basis of both the possibility and the necessity of humanity's religious experience. But this presence is such that the ego can neither fully exhaust its wealth and truth nor resist its compelling attractiveness and attendant urge to approach it and consciously assimilate its meaning. Thus the mandala, as interpreted by Jung, is an image of radical divine immanence which grounds a sense of transcendence in the individual psyche, even as it drives the ego toward unity with its divine center.

Jung came to this view not only through his study of Eastern religions, which often make use of mandalas in meditation and other rituals; it is based also on his empirical observation that mandala images arise spontaneously in the dreams and drawings of clinically "neurotic" individuals whose sense of identity is threatened—that is, they compensate the potential disintegration of the personality.

A conception of faith based on "mandalic consciousness," the idea of a creative center in the psyche which gives birth to all points of opposition on the circumference of human consciousness, would be much less of a threat to the continuation of humanity than a faith which identifies one point on the circumference as absolute and exhaustive of the circle's possibilities—which is in effect what the monotheisms do. The possessor of a mandalic faith experience would have no difficulty in acknowledging the immediate presence of the Absolute (called God, the Self or anything else) to every human life. Secure in this personal experience, the holder of such a faith could appreciate the form given to this universal presence by the tradition into which one was born, and seek its needed complementarity in other traditions with no sense of disloyalty. Perhaps most importantly, one could also see clearly the necessarily destructive implications for humanity of claims to exclusive and exhaustive revelation made by any one tradition. Such a faith, indeed, would make it possible to appreciate various and conflicting religious views, as relative yet valuable expressions of humanity's God-creating propensity. As other religions came to constitute no threat to one's own, the need to kill or convert would be broken in principle.

There is another saving feature of mandalic consciousness. In Jung's view the mandala not only depicts God as a circle whose center is everywhere and circumference nowhere (as in Bonaventure's allegory), it also focuses on the center as the midpoint between opposites. Such imagery highlights the binary nature of reality; it implies that reality is made up of opposites and that the investment of one's energy or life in one or other of the opposites leads to one-sidedness, which in psychological terms is a hallmark of neurosis. This could be taken to mean that any specific revelation should look to its opposite for its completion. The genuinely final revelation would then be the one in which a centered consciousness could relate empathically to all the contradictory revelations that have both graced and bloodied history, without identifying with any of them. This may be another way of saying that an adherence to any currently available tradition awaits its transcendence in a religious consciousness much richer and more encompassing than any that has yet manifested.

If Jung's reading of the psyche is correct—that individual and humanity are in fact being led to this consciousness by the deepest movements of the psyche itself—then his psychology does indeed hold out a hopeful vision to a humanity deeply wounded by its many faiths, and on the brink of destroying itself through them. From a Jungian perspective, even the winner of a religious war is defeated—by losing the compensating truth of the vanquished. Were the impulses of a mandalic consciousness to become more widespread, contending factions might be able to stop expending so much energy on the attempt to destroy, in the name of faith, those they don't agree with. Thus might be reversed the strange propensity of humanity to kill in order to preserve and extend the limitations of any particular faith.

It would be naive to believe that such mandalic consciousness lies within easy human reach. To achieve it would involve accepting the relative nature of currently constrictive religious and political orthodoxies. But paradoxically, the conditions of consciousness that in principle are capable of mitigating humanity's self-destructiveness continue to be seen by the leaders of political and religious orthodoxies as the ultimate form of heresy, a dangerous threat to the substance of the revelations entrusted to their care. Thus the freeing and fecund powers of doubt are constantly repressed.

Breaking these forms of possessive unconsciousness and the truncated and conflicting faiths they breed would require a radical re-examination of all claims to absolutism, especially as they appear in prophetic and millenarian expression. The collective mind of humanity would have to become capable of discerning what power possesses the prophet, and so see more clearly the possessive and manipulative components of his or her appeal. Such movements as "liberation theology" could then take the form of liberation *from* theology, since theology too can so easily become an archetypally empowered ideology. The prophetic call to enrage or depress a people would be met by a more conscious response, better insulated against the threat of unconscious manipulation by the power of the prophet's vision. Humanity could become more sensitive to its psycho-spiritual erogenous zones, and so come to treat those who manipulate these sensitivities in much the same way as it does those who take liberties with the body. As Jung remarks, "Wherever unconsciousness reigns, there is bondage and possession."[143]

These are but a few of the potential consequences of the widespread development of mandalic consciousness. Because it would understand faith as a universal propensity, faith could come to be seen as humanity's greatest gift and at the same time the greatest threat to its existence. Such an awareness could look gracefully on all historical expressions of faith, and yet be reluctant to terminate the process of the full unfolding of historical faith by taking one or other of its partial expressions as final. Thus doubt in the adequacy of any current religious configuration to meet the full range of human religious need would become the mother of hope in a movement toward a more adequate and potentially less destructive human religiosity. The spirit of this consciousness is captured in Jung's observation that the many gods became one and then that one became man:

> The gods at first lived in superhuman power and beauty on the top of snow-clad mountains or in the darkness of caves, woods and seas. Later on they drew together into one god, and then that god became man.[144]

These words can be read to mean that the current monotheisms could still be helpful, if seen as projections of the most significant religious movements of the human soul. The collective religious task now is to internalize these projections, and in so doing to see both their universal and yet relative truth. This approach would be able to appreciate these projections while allaying the tendency for one to destroy another through claims to its total truth.

In the spirit of such an understanding of religious reality, theologians could cease battling for the preservation of their lesser faiths; nor need they mourn their loss, but could begin to work cooperatively in the laying of the foundations for a greater, more encompassing faith, one more capable of guaranteeing the future of mankind. The basis of this faith, in Jung's estimate, is in the movement of the human psyche itself toward patterns of ever more inclusive empathies. Such a faith would realize that God needs many statements to bring the truth of humanity and divinity to full consciousness. Such a consciousness could not only embrace the truth of contradictory revelations but even recognize them as needful in the process of the mutual completion of the divine and the human.

Already, in many areas of human sensitivity, there is dawning the awareness that if the revelations currently available to humanity exhaust the divine capacity, then this capacity is peculiarly impoverished and somehow less than that of the human imagination it claims to address with finality. The faith emerging through these sensitivities is richer, more variegated, more at ease with itself and both surer and more critical of its suppositions; as such it is much less vulnerable to the convictions and compulsions that so easily become holocaustic. It is closer to that sense of wholeness which according to Jung is intended for mankind by the ultimate sponsor of consciousness —the Self or God within.

Desirable as all this might appear, it may yet constitute too great a challenge for the Western religious mind. This is so because it would mean accepting that the individual is naturally imbued with a latent divinity. As Jung writes, "the 'God within' presents a dogmatic difficulty" to mainstream Christian theology.[145] Jung's thesis would in fact extend the Chalcedonian view of Christ as two natures in one person—a human and a divine—to a description of the teleological movement of any human life, which is to say that psychic maturity resides in the discovery of one's native divinity.

In this sense Jung argues that the split between the human and the divine has never been acceptable to the unconscious, which therefore periodically erupts in the individual and in the collective to reassert the natural and universal continuity between humanity and its divine origins.[146] If orthodox religion could accept this view, the figure of Christ (for instance) would not be presented as historically unique, a dogmatic position which alienates human beings rather than attracts them, for it makes a monster of the Christ figure to hold that one is only human in the presence of the one human who was also divine. Jung's Christology, on the other hand, is profoundly appreciative of the truth of the Christian myth—as peculiarly capable of depicting universal movements in the psyche—while avoiding the literalism and historicism that makes the Christ event only a discrete reality in space and time, which severs believers from its truth in their immediate experience of themselves.

A second major obstacle to the emergence of mandalic consciousness is the social implications of such a position. It is difficult to deny that the general thrust of Jung's thought gives a certain precedence to personal transformation over collective transformation; that is, all change, of whatever scope, proceeds from what happens within the individual. No doubt one could present compelling reasons why it is better or healthier to be a Christian lemming than a Marxist lemming, or vice versa. But Jung's quest and hope was for life beyond lemminghood. In the face of conventional religious rhetoric which speaks of a people set apart—the chosen, pastors and their flocks—Jung affirms that more humane and harmonious social structures derive from, rather than lead to, a more harmonious self-relatedness. Hence militant socialism, fascism or capitalism was no more attractive to Jung than any other rampant "ism."

In the final analysis, Jung believes that only a numinous contact with the Self—always an individual, as opposed to individualistic, event—can allay the sheepish mentality that inevitably results from immersing one's identity in collective consciousness. When the bond between ego and Self is severed, the individual is lost.[147] This bond, in Jung's view, is made most tenuous when the individual's sense of personal divinity and attendant dignity is projected onto an external God, religious or ideological, and through the attendant loss of self-identity in the collective worship of this projection. Such a process describes the loss of responsible consciousness in members of the various religious and political flocks pitted against one another in the service of archetypal powers; the faith these powers elicit now threatens to terminate in one final, holocaustic "revelation."

If these powers are not to destroy the humanity from whose depths they proceed, it must become more sensitive to their reality and to their ineradicable presence in the human psyche. In this process of becoming sensitive, Jung's thought on the genesis of the Gods, their revelations and the faith they engender has far-reaching implications for the survival of humanity. For he can show that all are partial statements of eternal truth, that none exhaust it, and that the power which gives birth to them all works ultimately for their synthesis— providing the conflicting urgencies attached to each partial expression do not lead to a premature and irrevocable termination of the whole process.

It would be a significant step toward survival if every discipline concerned with life on earth were to seriously examine, in concert, Jung's conception of a personal and historical Self intrinsic to the life of the psyche, an inner center capable of bringing the Gods and Goddesses it unleashes on humanity into configurations of greater harmony, wealth of being and consciousness. Should such a psychic reality prove not to exist after all, or should humanity fail to bring its power to consciousness, humanity would seem destined to continue to wait for its redemption through the intervention of an extrinsic deity.

Given the enmity bred between and within the traditions historically spawned by such "divine" interventions, and given humanity's current technological capacity to destroy itself, this wait may now be short.

7

Of Sheep and Shepherds: Pastoral
Psychology and the Psychology of Pastors

*So far as I can see, no relevant objection could be
raised from the Christian point of view against
anyone accepting the task of individuation imposed
on us by nature, and the recognition of our
wholeness or completeness, as a binding personal
commitment.*
—C.G. Jung[148]

Jung's critique of Christianity and his views on the current
state of monotheistic consciousness have important implications for both pastors and the practice of pastoral psychology.

Pastors serve as the leaders of Christian communities. As
such, they are charged with the implementation of Christian
dogma, its ritual celebration and its attendant social and ethical values. How effectively and with what degree of personal
integrity can they do this if the Christian myth is understood
by both pastor and flock as unrelated to the individual human
psyche?

In a variety of ways Jung is saying that too often the truth
contained in the Christian myth remains foreign to the life of
the psyche. It is presented as deriving from a source beyond
life, rather than from the deepest movements of psychic life
which gave birth to the myth. Such a view is often justified by
such theological categories as supernaturalism or the sinfulness of man.

The removal of the Christian myth from its origins in the
human psyche turns the myth into an ideology inimical to the
humanity it could enlighten and invigorate. The dynamic of

this transition hinges on the presupposition that the myth derives from a transcendent God and that the intellectual acceptance of it, in spite of what Jung calls its "sacrosanct unintelligibility," is somehow connected with human salvation. Thus both pastor and flock can become panicked into a violation of their humanity through a forced acceptance of a reality extraneous to it. As the myth becomes institutionalized, many careers and other vested interests become attached to the promulgation of such alienated consciousness and so the panic continues.

Jung's suggestion to pastor and flock alike is that recognition of the Christian themes as statements grounded in the movements of the psyche would alleviate the need for the pastor to impose a foreign body of thought and practice on his flock, and relieve the flock of the need to accept such a burden. In this way the mutual patterns of unfreedom, if not actual exploitation, that can come to exist between shepherd and sheep would be diminished. Both could look to the resonance of the myth in their own immediate experience of themselves; in their own depths they could find the meaning of the myth, the moral imperative attached to it and also the authority with which it is to be implemented in their lives as believers.

In a piece of amateurish or playful sociology, Jung once sought to answer a question put to him by leaders of the Swiss Christian Students' Conference—whether people in spiritual distress preferred to consult a doctor or a clergyman. He sent around a questionnaire which was answered by Swiss, German and French Protestants, and a few Catholics:

> Those who decided for the doctor represented 57 per cent of the Protestants and only 25 per cent of the Catholics, while those who decided for the clergyman formed only 8 percent of the Protestants as against 58 per cent of the Catholics. These were the unequivocal decisions. The remaining 35 per cent of the Protestants could not make up their minds, while only 17 per cent of the Catholics were undecided.
>   .... Curiously enough, there was even one clergyman who decided for the doctor, while another made the irritated retort:

"Theology has nothing to do with the treatment of human beings." All the relatives of clergymen who answered my questionnaire pronounced themselves against the clergy.[149]

The main reason given for not consulting the clergyman, writes Jung, was "his lack of psychological knowledge and insight."[150]

This was more than fifty years ago, and not at all a "scientific" sampling, but what it revealed does not fly in the face of general experience even today. The organic connection Jung's work seeks to establish between the revealed and human words and worlds is still heretical to those who cannot accept the unconscious origins of faith.

The acceptance of Jung's views by the Christian community could have many positive results. It would, for instance, relieve the pastoral theologian or psychologist from having to bend the psychological breakthroughs of the last century to the needs of a revealed ideology. If it were acknowledged that psychological, spiritual and revelatory experience proceed to consciousness from a common source, there would be no need to tailor psychological experience to the needs of orthodoxy—especially where orthodox views are a major obstacle to maturity. Such an awareness would be more comfortable with the idea that religious and psychological experience are organically one.

With this realization theology would be forced to forsake its ideological character. Theologian and pastor could come to see the revelation they adhere to in terms of their own experience of themselves and the movements of their lives. They could then be more at home with the so-called inbreaking Word of God. Such "inbreaking" might then share less of the intrusive and disruptive nature of neurosis—or more severe psychological complaints, where the words of a variety of Gods and Goddesses actually burst in with devastating consequences to the personality. This newly found ease with their own inner treasure could also lead more pastoral theologians and psychologists to appreciate the religious treasures of other Words from other Gods.

To the extent that this ground unity of psychic and revela-tory experience is denied, the split between psychology and religion, between the human and the divine, should be frankly admitted. Theologies that take this tack should not pretend, in their dialogue with developmental psychology, that they have anything to contribute to or derive from the various move-ments concerned with human potential. Holding the view that the only hope for mankind lies in a transcendent God neither ontologically nor epistemologically continuous with human consciousness, such inorganic theologies must concede that they can have nothing to do with a conception of human potential which 1) identifies the experience of God as the most valuable natural endowment of the psyche, and 2) con-tends that the intensification of this experience is functionally identical with the process of psychic, and so spiritual and human, maturation.

In this respect Jung's psychology could be used to identify those theologies which have within them the resources to heal the breach between psychological experience and maturity, on the one hand, and religious experience and theological reflec-tion upon it, on the other. Theologies that deliberately breach the natural continuity between divine and human would not qualify as bearers of an organic consciousness capable of uni-fying psychic and religious experience. Most Western theolo-gies, unfortunately, are in one way or another dedicated to the maintenance of this breach.

Theologies built on an absolute and discontinuous disjunc-tion between the natural and the supernatural can never, in principle, promote the organic connection between divine and human that Jung understands as integral to psychological ma-turity. When divinity is defined as extrinsic to the human psyche, the individual caught by such a theology is required to submit to external authorities. These usually manifest to the individual through authoritarian systems based on hierarchies of power, or traditional books of wisdom purveying revela-tions deemed final. The individual thus caught is not likely to look to his or her interiority as the place of origin of whatever religious truth these external authorities seek to convey or impose. Nor is such inner searching encouraged.

The same criticism applies to the notion of God as "wholly other." If God is so in principle, then he must remain so in practice; having no aspect of being in common with humanity, his intervention in human life cannot but be intrusive. Among theologians, Paul Tillich's thought in this respect is particularly acute. He points out that a wholly other God, in a revelatory or redemptive approach to mankind, would destroy the structures he had created if he were ontologically discontinuous with his creation:

> Miracles cannot be interpreted in terms of a supranatural interference in natural processes. If such an interpretation were true, the manifestation of the ground of being would destroy the structure of being; God would be split within himself, as religious dualism has asserted. It would be more adequate to call such a miracle "demonic."[151]

Another variant of the attempted eradication of the divine in the human is the theologically popular conception of human corruption or total sinfulness. In Jung's view this doctrine is the ultimate debasement of the soul's natural divine dignity. In such theologies the degree of sinfulness of the soul is in direct correlation to the turning of consciousness from its inner connectedness with God to an expected salvation from without. The worthlessness of the human is directly proportioned to the intensity with which salvation is sought from beyond, usually mediated through the appropriate ecclesiastical agency. Such views not only divorce consciousness from its proximity to God, they also become a foundational justification for redemptive institutions. By cutting off the individual's access to the life-giving powers of his or her interiority, and by turning the search for salvation from an inner journey into a search for an external transcendent, such theologies, however sophisticated they may be, reduce hope to the status of a cargo cult.

A movement to assimilate Jung's perception of the organic unity of psychic and religious experience could overcome the foreign-to-life quality that adheres to an unintelligible "Good News." The good news that is Christ, when clung to with a faith that simply wills an assent to the meaningless, threatens to become bad news. The synthesis of life and religion as it is promoted in Jung's thought could alleviate the split consciousness that currently characterizes the mind of pastor and flock. Among pastors it could reverse the ever increasing flow from altars of ordination to detoxification and rehabilitation centers —a flow which must surely prompt one to ponder the effect of the good news on so many of its modern bearers. Among the flock it could stem the movement toward lives of spiritual emptiness.

If it is true that theologians and their followers too often need professional and so-called secular help in order to recover from the consequences of their theology, it would involve the Church these theologians serve in a strange paradox. Such an institution would presumably be forced, in all justice, to provide the healing services necessary for those injured by its disciplines and dogma. It is of course to the credit of the institutional Church that it is sponsoring numerous agencies throughout the land dedicated to the healing of those hurt by it—especially its leaders. However, it is difficult to escape the conclusion that a situation in which so many need healing from their healers, and salvation from their saviors, should be addressed in depth and reversed in principle. A major factor in this reversal would be the acceptance of a more organic relationship between *psyche* and *theos*. The experience of this connection would point to the natural unity of the sacred and the psychic as the precondition for a less lethal adherence to one or other of the specific faiths.

Jung proffers at least three different scenarios in which the connection between a commitment to a faith and the relation to the unconscious can be understood. In the first scenario religion is a functionally effective component of an individual's life. When this is the case, religious beliefs and practices serve as a valuable, external aid for the believer's sustained contact with the unconscious—even though the individual may remain unconscious of the process involved. What Jung means here is that when the flow of energies between ego and unconscious is adequate to the demands of life, the psyche is best left undisturbed by a more deliberate or conscious approach to the unconscious.[152] Indeed, Jung states that in certain cases where he judged a solution to psychological problems to be institutionally or sacramentally available, he would direct people away from analysis and to the healing resources of their specific tradition. For instance he would suggest that Catholics avail themselves of confession as an alternative to embarking on a full-fledged analysis.[153] And in a talk given in 1939 he implies that the access to the unconscious provided through the Catholic sacramental and ritual tradition—even though this access itself be unconscious in many cases—tends to diminish the incidence of neurosis among followers of that tradition.[154]

The position Jung takes here illumines not only the limitations and conditions he himself would set for the pastoral use of his psychology. It also illustrates quite clearly his understanding of the nature of religion and the experience which grounds it. Religion is for Jung the experience arising from a sustained and energy-giving contact with the unconscious. Institutional religions exist for the purpose of mediating this experience. Where they do so successfully, Jung appears willing to let sleeping dogs lie, so to speak. It is only where they largely or wholly fail to provide satisfactory mediation that a direct and conscious relationship with the unconscious is demanded; and this demand is made by the psyche itself in the interest of spiritual health.

This kind of thinking lies behind the importance Jung attaches to the restoration of an appreciation for what he calls the symbolic life. He would have the churches themselves acknowledge the symbolic life as an expression of the unconscious. In Jung's view the recovery of the symbolic sense, and the sensitivity to the unconscious involved in this process, would enable the churches to again experience the vitality of their symbols and so enhance their capacity to mediate something of this vitality to the surrounding culture.

However, for the reasons outlined above, Christianity has historically moved further and further from these sensitivities, often through deliberate theological options. Cut off from the inner life that originally gave birth to its symbols and that should be mediated by them, the Christian myth has more and more become simply a hollow container. It is not surprising, then, that fewer people find satisfaction in it.

This brings us to Jung's second scenario, which applies to an ongoing relationship between a formal religious faith and the analytic process. Here he depicts a situation in which an experience of the unconscious, when mediated by analysis, could result in an individual's return to his or her religious tradition with an intensified appreciation of its spiritual symbols and resources.[155] In such cases the analytic experience may interact with the religious experience in such a way as to renew and then to intensify the individual's relationship with the prior religious tradition. One's formal religious experience and one's psychic experience can coalesce into configurations approximating unity, or can at least reach an interface where they support, enliven and deepen each other. Religious and psychological growth could thereby approach an identity beyond the too frequent opposition that currently prevails.

In such a psycho-spiritual situation, it is conceivable that the believer's adherence to a specific set of symbols would be not only intensified, but also enlarged and so alleviated by an appreciation of their relativity due to the personal experience of the ground of all symbol systems in the psyche.[156]

A third discernible scenario, which seems to be becoming more prevalent today, is one in which Jung sees a re-commitment to a previous religious tradition as no longer viable, because it would constitute an unacceptable compromise with the demands of psychic maturation. The best illustration in Jung's work of such a situation is the case of the physicist Wolfgang Pauli.[157] In his commentary on Pauli's material,

Jung reads certain of his dreams to indicate that a return to his childhood Catholicism would be an evasion of the rigors involved in his individuation.[158] In Jung's opinion there was "no going home" in this case and, by implication, in any psycho-spiritual situation where an attempted return to a long abandoned religious tradition would no longer honestly meet the demands of spiritual maturity. In such situations one must face the reality of the divine intent directly, that is as it reveals itself in the immediate expressions of the unconscious, without the benefit of ecclesiastical mediation.

Clearly, however, a conscious relationship with the unconscious is not in principle hostile to a committed religious faith. In fact, from a Jungian perspective there are few instances in which a believing individual or community, unless their beliefs seriously inhibit balanced growth, need fear the unconscious or contact with it. More likely a connection with one's own unconscious would intensify one's appreciation of the religious depths inherent in all aspects of life. From the secure standpoint of personal experience one can both value the impact of one's own religious tradition and see its limitations. This can lead to a much more differentiated appreciation of religious beliefs in general, including an openness to the relative truths expressed in books of wisdom other than those revered by one's own religious tradition.

Only when an individual, for a host of possible reasons, has turned away from the symbolic life as mediated through the tradition into which one was born, or only when the tradition has alienated its followers from the life it purports to mediate, must one face the divine reality more directly. Only in this latter and very specific case would the analytic process function as a substitute for the living of a religious life in a more conventional or traditional way. Though this may be an option into which more are currently being forced, it is not one over which Jung rejoices, since it means that too often the analytic process must provide a function that the churches have in fact abdicated.

There is in Jung's work considerable support for arguing

that those in positions of giving sustained spiritual direction to others should experience the truth of the unconscious through a personal analysis.[159] However, he does deplore, at times strongly, the fact that the churches have lost access to the depths of the human soul and spirit, as expressed in symbol and acted out in rite. An ideal implicit in his thought would be the emergence within Christianity of a conscious appreciation of the unconscious origin of symbols.

The fact that too often the analyst, and the analytic approach, must step in to provide what specifically Christian mediation does not, remains for Jung a testimony to Christianity's current impoverishment—in no small part responsible for the illness that we are.

8

The Gnostic Christian

*Disparagement and vilification of Gnosticism are
an anachronism. Its obviously psychological
symbolism could serve many people today as a
bridge to a more living appreciation of Christian
tradition.*

—C.G. Jung[160]

In the final analysis, both Jung's appreciation and his criticism
of the Christian myth derive from his personal experience of
what he came to call the collective unconscious. Jung was
convinced that what he had experienced in himself was the
basis in humanity for all so-called religious experience. Moreover he came to feel that the movement or teleology of the
religion-making energies of the unconscious was toward personal and collective wholeness.

In the light of his experience and subsequent research, Jung
was able to appreciate Christianity as a powerful archetypal
compensation and gift to mankind, and he not infrequently
deplored its diminished significance in modern consciousness.
"For it seems to me," he writes in his essay on the Trinity,
"that the world, if it should lose sight of these archetypal
statements, would be threatened with unspeakable impoverishment of mind and soul."[161]

But in light of the same experience Jung was able to identify Christianity as only one significant expression of the unconscious among many, and further to show its limitations in
terms of the compensation it offered to contemporary, collective consciousness. Conceding that Christianity originally had
to be one-sided toward the spiritual and away from the in-

stinctual, given the then prevailing social situation, he maintained that now the balance had swung the other way.

Jung's position, when read in its totality, would thus call for a new compensation, which in the logic of his own thought might itself have to bear the power of revelation. This is what could balance the one-sidedness of the Christian myth, without at the same time sacrificing the historical gains in consciousness already made.

One interesting and lively option for the regaining of the balance needed within Christianity would be the re-appropriation and assimilation of those movements of the spirit which Christianity, in the interests of its own survival, has historically been forced to declare heretical. With this in mind, Jung's thought challenges orthodox Christian theologies to embark on the recovery of truths it has hitherto felt obliged to reject. This is what must be done, in Jung's view, if Christianity is to come into possession of a conception of humanity and human spirituality that is more appropriate to the psychological process of becoming whole.

The two major areas of recovery which Jung's thought insists upon are a sense of mankind's native divinity and the value of the body in the interplay between body and spirit. On a deeper level, where he explores those unities sometimes described as pertaining to mystical forms of experience, the spirit of Jung's writings implies that these two areas are ultimately one. For the intersection of the ego with its source in its psychic depths would give birth to a consciousness totally accepting of all aspects of the human. Thus the power of centering—to which Jung alludes when he describes the Self as a *spiritus rector,* a rectifying spirit—would be the power of God, experienced in the depths of one's being, bringing together such opposites as body and spirit in the interest of those harmonies and unities this inner God demands.

Jung found an image for this process in the Gnostic figure of Christ, which "symbolizes man's original unity and exalts it as the saving goal of his development"; this "saving goal" is described by Jung as follows:

By "composing the unstable," by bringing order into chaos, by resolving disharmonies and centering upon the mid-point, thus setting a "boundary" to the multitude and focusing attention upon the cross, consciousness is reunited with the unconscious, the unconscious man is made one with his center, which is also the center of the universe, and in this wise the goal of man's salvation and exaltation is reached.[162]

The need to re-establish the human psyche as the *temenos* or container in which the divine-human encounter takes place was the basis of Jung's early attraction to the Gnostic writings. Though he admits he never found in Gnosticism the psychic intelligibility he later discovered in alchemy, he saw there expressions of the experience of God which he interpreted as movement through levels of the psyche to its sacred center. In the face of a Christianity which has almost entirely lost this experience, or even the possibility of conceiving of it through its shallow theological anthropology, Jung calls for a return to the Gnostic sense of God as an inner, directing presence.

From this point of view, the argument could be made that if Christianity is not to be trivialized through literalism and historicism—who saved the cosmos by rising from the dead in 33 A.D.?—it must regain that Gnostic sense of the Christian mysteries which locates their truth in the movement of the human soul or psyche. Similarly, Paul Tillich speaks of the need for a restored Christian *gnosis*, with an *amor intellectualis*, an intellectual love, as its feeling tone.[163]

This state of being in which thinking and feeling are unified, and grounded in a sense of one's immediate participation in the divine, is very close to the Gnostic experience, and one which was apparently natural to Jung himself. "Suddenly I understood," he writes, recalling his childhood years, "that God was, for me at least, one of the most certain and immediate of experiences."[164] He alludes to it as sustaining him in the clerical atmosphere of his home, where there was much talk of God by his minister father, but apparently no personal experience of what was being talked about:

When I heard him preaching about grace, I always thought of my own experience. What he said sounded stale and hollow, like a tale told by someone who knows it only by hearsay and cannot quite believe it himself.[165]

Jung's emphasis on dreams as a means of personal revelation is significant in this context, for such a view would re-open, in a Gnostic-Christian perspective, the question of canonical truth. It would do this by relating the individual to his or her dreams and the accompanying myth they reveal as one's personal canon.

Instead of considering revelation to be somehow over and done with, ending with the historical closing of the canon, a psychological perspective would understand revelation to continue in the individual dialogue between ego and unconscious. The New Testament or Covenant would cease to be a once-upon-a-time contract whose terms are spelled out in sacred texts. Rather a genuinely *new* testament would be struck every time the individual was led by the Self into dialogue with it, in the interests of its (the Self's) more conscious incarnation. As this process developed, one would be in a better position to relate one's own testament to the biblical New Testament, through a more immediate contact with the source of both—the human psyche.

Again, unless one's Christianity were hostile to the potential value of more balanced and extensive empathies, it is difficult to see how the discovery of one's personal, new and renewing testament could be in serious conflict with the underlying intent of *the* New Testament.

As such a consciousness developed, the individual possessing it would be in a better position to know what within any given religious tradition was in the best interests of his or her spiritual development. An intensified sense of one's personal truth would free the churches to play the role of spiritual servants, a role they have long laid dubious claim to. For instance, Catholics would feel free to understand and use sacramental activity as an externalization of the deepest movements of the psyche; this activity would facilitate their fuller participation in the life of the psyche, but in the manner and at the pace dictated by the Self addressing them personally, through the unconscious, in the specifics of their life at any given moment.

Undifferentiated and universal spiritual directives or moral advice would come to be seen as inappropriate, even manipulative or coercive—unless such norms were themselves more obviously qualified by a sensitivity to the manner in which the divine addresses the life of the individual from one's personal depths. Similarly, both Reform and Catholic Christians could listen to the Word of God not only as it sounds in the event of Jesus, but as it sounds too in the personal revelations that manifest in the meaning of dreams or however else the unconscious announces its intent for the individual.

The second major compensation badly needed by Christianity, according to Jung, was the restoration of a sense of body. Here Jung turned more to the alchemical tradition than to the Gnostics, whose spirit, at least in certain of their writings, can be understood as sharing, if not intensifying, the Christian's flight from the material world.

Jung was of the opinion that the late medieval alchemists were involved in the search for a spirituality in which body and soul were integrated, one in which the spirit of Mercurius, with its robust vitality and fire, might provide what was missing in the more pallid Christianity of the time. In this area Jung's thought poses the question of why the Christian spirit should turn to alchemy if its own teachings were adequate to the needs of the soul. Why look for the Philosophers' Stone in an effort to evolve the *aurum non vulgus,* the "true gold" of consciousness, if traditional Christian spirituality could effect the *opus?*

If Jung does take the position, as he seems to, that the mercurial spirit is a needed compensation for the one-sidedness of Christianity, much of the nature of this compensation has to do with the attitude toward the body and generally with engagement in the world. When he systematizes his perceptions about alchemy, drawing on the work of Gerhard Dorn, Jung speaks of an initial stage in the coveted *unio mentalis,* harshly ascetic and demanding, having as its goal the freeing of the soul from its bodily restrictions and compulsions:

> Their "spirit" was their own belief in the light—a spirit which drew the soul to itself from its imprisonment in the body; but the soul brought with it the darkness of the chthonic spirit, the unconscious. The separation was so important because the dark deeds of the soul had to be checked. The *unio mentalis* signified, therefore, an extension of consciousness and the governance of the soul's movements by the spirit of truth.[166]

This process, analogous psychologically to coming to terms with one's shadow, is not unlike Christian asceticism, and for the alchemists it apparently raised the same problem. "But since the soul made the body to live and was the principle of all realization," writes Jung, "the philosophers could not but see that after the separation the body and its world were dead."[167] Hence in the alchemical *opus* there is a second stage, one in which the soul previously freed is re-embodied and so prevented from a premature escape to eternal or heavenly realms.[168]

In this movement toward re-embodiment of the soul Jung implicitly locates the psychic truth of the symbol of resurrection, which would be nothing less than the transformation of consciousness that attaches to the process of becoming whole in the here and now of everyday life. Resurrection so understood would thus involve the state of conscious awareness consequent upon living a human life in increasing resonance with the source of that life in the psyche. This conception of resurrection removes it from the realm of extraordinary geriatrics and relocates it in the area of human spirituality. What Jung writes of the alchemists' search for a union of the opposites through "magical" procedures is available to everyone through assiduous attention to the demands of their own unconscious:

> The creation of unity by a magical procedure meant the possibility of effecting a union with the world—not with the world of multiplicity as we see it but with the potential world, the

eternal Ground of all empirical being, just as the self is the ground and origin of the individual personality past, present, and future.[169]

Only from the base of a thus embodied spirituality does Jung consider universal forms of perception and love to be authentic. The alchemical images of this process are often frankly sexual—as they also are in modern dreams and other products of the unconscious—pointing to the importance of sexuality as a simultaneously physical and spiritual reality. The sexual itself is viewed not with the traditional suspicion of Christian moralities distrustful of its mercurial power. Rather the sexual is understood as a sacrament of the spiritual.

Certain of the images in alchemical writings, for instance the male-female androgyne, point to the unity of the sexes in a single life process, symbol of the union of opposites that attaches to consciousness of the Self. This is a far cry from Christianity, whose metaphysics and morality remain all too capable of understanding sexuality as somehow accidental, if not incidental, to human being and human spirituality.

No wonder there are current shifts in individual and collective consciousness which view with suspicion theologies concocted by bachelor castes or by those whose God remains extrinsic to the psyche. These modern movements may be harbingers of a newly dawning and more adequate myth and spirituality. They may be the bearers of that humanizing compensation which Jung claimed contemporary Christianity cries out for under the overriding divine imperative for wholeness in history.

Jung's works abound in selections from Gnostics, mystics and alchemists, all of whom pointed to the God within, a sense of the divine that is capable of bringing body, soul and spirit into more wholesome harmonies. Much of his own writing rivets the reader to the page, rich with the compelling beauty of his spiritual vision. It is an enticing view of mankind's potential, borne of Jung's conviction of the inescapable nearness of the living God. This God, according to Jung, authors the conflicts in personal and collective life in order to complete itself in human life through more intensely lived and higher unities.

For the Christian to claim entry into the further reaches of Jung's vision without the painful—perhaps impossible—facing of the hitherto excluded Christian shadow would be to betray the ardor of his spirit for a cheaply gained wisdom and attenuated sense of the sacred. If we are to truly assimilate his message, then the reasons for our current spiritual truncation, the extent of our one-sidedness, and our prolonged and energetic fight against the divinely proferred wholeness which our nature demands must be faced in depth.

This will require what we all would rather avoid: sustained and soul-searching reflection on the illness that we are.

Notes

CW—*The Collected Works of C.G. Jung* (Bollingen Series XX). 20 vols. Trans. R.F.C. Hull. Ed. H. Read, M. Fordham, G. Adler, Wm. McGuire. Princeton: Princeton University Press, 1953-1979.

1. "Psychological Commentary on *The Tibetan Book of the Great Liberation,*" *Psychology and Religion: West and East,* CW 11, par. 779.
2. See *Psychology and Alchemy,* CW 12, par. 9. Though this position underlies all Jung's mature thought, it is explicit when he writes here: "It is a telling fact that two theological reviewers of my book *Psychology and Religion*—one of them Catholic, the other Protestant—assiduously overlooked my demonstration of the psychic origin of religious phenomena."
3. See *C.G. Jung Letters,* ed. G. Adler and A. Jaffé (Bollingen Series XCV; Princeton: Princeton University Press, 1973-1975), vol. 2, pp. 6, 21, 84, 89, 97, 157, 275.
4. "A Psychological Approach to the Dogma of the Trinity," *Psychology and Religion,* CW 11, par. 170.
5. "Psychological Commentary on *The Tibetan Book of the Great Liberation,*" ibid., par. 779. Note that Jung consistently equates the experience of wholeness with the experience of God, and functionally equates the archetype of the Self with the drive to wholeness and with the God-image in the psyche: "It is only through the psyche that we can establish that God acts upon us, but we are unable to distinguish whether these actions emanate from God or from the unconscious.... Both are border-line concepts for transcendental contents." ("Answer to Job," ibid., par. 757)
6. "A Psychological Approach to the Dogma of the Trinity," ibid., par. 171.
7. Jung does, however, attempt to give some definition to what he means by religion and its relation to creed, dogma, myth and rite. ("Psychology and Religion," ibid., pars. 9f, 81f)
8. For instance: "But one thing is certain—that modern man, Protestant or otherwise, has lost the protection of ecclesiastical walls erected and reinforced so carefully since Roman days, and because of this loss has approached the zone of world-creating fire." (Ibid., par. 84)

101

9. Ibid., par. 86.

10. Ibid., pars. 33f. See also "Answer to Job," where Jung writes (and this is a typical sentiment): "It [Protestantism] seems to have succumbed to a species of rationalistic historicism and to have lost any understanding of the Holy Ghost who works in the hidden places of the soul. It can neither understand nor admit a further revelation of the divine drama." (Ibid., par. 749)

11. *C.G. Jung Letters,* vol. 2, p. 9. See also his remarks in "Answer to Job": "The logical consistency of the papal declaration [the Assumption of Mary] cannot be surpassed, and leaves Protestantism with the odium of being nothing but a *man's religion* which allows no metaphysical representation of woman." (*Psychology and Religion,* CW 11, par. 753)

12. "Psychology and Religion," ibid., par. 76. The same point is made more directly when he criticizes the Protestant dismissal of symbol and rite: "With the demolition of the protective walls, the Protestant lost the sacred images that expressed important unconscious factors, together with the ritual which, from time immemorial, has been a safe way of dealing with the unpredictable forces of the unconscious." (Ibid., par. 82)

13. See "Why I Am Not a Catholic," *The Symbolic Life,* CW 18, especially pars. 1466ff.

14. "A Psychological Approach to the Dogma of the Trinity," *Psychology and Religion,* CW 11, par. 285.

15. Ibid., par. 170.

16. *Symbols of Transformation,* CW 5, par. 336.

17. Ibid.

18. "Psychology and Religion," *Psychology and Religion,* CW 11, par. 102.

19. See, for example, "A Psychological Approach to the Dogma of the Trinity," ibid., par. 178: "The archetype is 'that which is believed always, everywhere, and by everybody.'"

20. The bulk of Jung's work in these areas is collected in the articles that make up the volume *Psychology and Religion: West and East,* CW 11.

21. "Psychology and Religion," ibid., par. 100.

22. *Mysterium Coniunctionis,* CW 14, par. 675.

23. "Psychological Commentary on *The Tibetan Book of the Great Liberation,*" *Psychology and Religion,* CW 11, pars. 770-771. The same point is made in ibid., par. 779, referred to above (notes 1 and 5).

24. In a letter written on June 8, 1942, Jung praises Paracelsus as "one of the most outstanding exponents of a spiritual movement which sought to reverse this turning away from our psychic origins as a result of Scholasticism and Aristotelianism." (*C.G. Jung Letters*, vol. 1, p. 317)

25. Ibid., p. 318.

26. See Jung's descriptive definition of enantiodromia in *Psychological Types*, CW 6, par. 708, and his references to it in *Two Essays on Analytical Psychology*, CW 7, par. 111.

27. *Symbols of Transformation*, CW 5, par. 104.

28. This is one of the central motifs in Jung's series of essays on the symbolism of the fish, in *Aion*, CW 9ii.

29. "Symbols cannot be produced intentionally.... They grow out of the individual or collective unconscious and cannot function without being accepted by the unconscious dimension of our being." [Paul Tillich, *The Dynamics of Faith* (New York: Harper & Row, 1958), p. 43] He makes the same point in "The Nature of Religious Language," *Theology of Culture* (Oxford: Oxford University Press, 1959), where he writes: "'Out of what womb are symbols born?' Out of the womb which is usually called today the 'group unconscious' or 'collective unconscious,' or whatever you want to call it. Out of a group which acknowledges in this thing, this word, this flag, or whatever it may be, its own being." (p. 58)

30. See John P. Dourley, *The Psyche as Sacrament: A Comparative Study of C.G. Jung and Paul Tillich* (Toronto: Inner City Books, 1981), pp. 73ff.

31. See, for instance, Elaine Pagels, *The Gnostic Gospels* (New York: Random House, 1979), which is particularly incisive and representative of research in the field of Gnosticism. The connections she draws with psychoanalytic theory and with Jung's interpretation of gnosis (pp. 126, 133f) are provocative, and although too concise, they appear in principle to be open to a much more elaborate and sophisticated development.

32. *Psychology and Alchemy*, CW 12, par. 10.

33. In his autobiographical *Memories, Dreams, Reflections* (New York: Vintage Books, 1961), Jung describes his search for the historical precedents of his own experience (pp. 200f); he found them remotely in the Gnostic tradition, but more immediately in medieval alchemy, the connecting link between Gnosticism and the modern age.

34. Jung's work contains many references to Jacob Boehme, Meister Eckhart, Bonaventure, Angelus Silesius and others whom

he considered to be mystics; that is, they had a lively contact with the unconscious.

35. Jung's major writings on alchemy are *Psychology and Alchemy,* CW 12; *Alchemical Studies,* CW 13; and *Mysterium Coniunctionis,* CW 14. See also Marie-Louise von Franz, *Alchemy: An Introduction to the Symbolism and the Psychology* (Toronto: Inner City Books, 1980).

36. See *Psychological Types,* CW 6, par. 733, where Jung compares Plato to Kant as follows: "Plato sees the idea as a prototype of things, while Kant defines it as the 'archetype [*Urbild*] of all practical employment of reason,' a transcendental concept which as such exceeds the bounds of the experienceable."

37. "Greek natural philosophy with its interest in matter, together with Aristotelian reasoning, has achieved a belated but overwhelming victory over Plato." (*The Archetypes and the Collective Unconscious,* CW 9i, par. 149)

38. See "Psychological Commentary on *The Tibetan Book of the Dead,*" *Psychology and Religion,* CW 11, par. 785 and "The Psychology of Eastern Meditation," ibid., par. 908.

39. See Paul Tillich, "The Two Types of Philosophy of Religion," *Theology of Culture,* pp. 16-19.

40. In response to the Thomistic conception of the existence of God, Tillich writes: "It is obvious that this second concept of existence brings God's existence down to the level of that of a stone or a star, and it makes atheism not only possible, but almost unavoidable, as the latter development has proved." (Ibid., p. 18) Again, writing about the type of consciousness involved in objectifying and proving God's existence, Tillich states: "To such a concept and to such attempts atheism is the right religious and theological reply." (Ibid., p. 28)

41. "The different answers given to this question [how *Deus* and *esse* relate] are milestones on the road of Western religious consciousness; and this road is a road toward ever-increasing *loss* of religious consciousness." (Ibid., p. 12)

42. *Symbols of Transformation,* CW 5, par. 622: "As Justin Martyr indignantly observes, the connections between the Christian legend and that of Dionysus are unmistakable (e.g., the miracle of the wine)." See also *Aion,* CW 9ii, pars. 267, 274.

43. *Alchemical Studies,* CW 13, par. 295.

44. *Mysterium Coniunctionis,* CW 14, par. 41. Here Jung refers to Bonaventure's *Itinerarium,* Chapter 5, for one formulation of this principle. He relates it to a religious description of the Self

in *Psychological Types,* CW 6, par. 791, note 74; and in "A Psychological Approach to the Dogma of the Trinity," *Psychology and Religion,* CW 11, par. 229, he relates the principle to Hermetic and Gnostic traditions and to the medieval thinker Alan de Lulle.

45. See "Concerning Mandala Symbolism," *The Archetypes and the Collective Unconscious,* CW 9i.

46. "Psychological Commentary on *The Tibetan Book of the Dead,*" *Psychology and Religion,* CW 11, par. 845: "As the products of imagination are always in essence visual, their forms must, from the outset, have the character of images, and moreover of *typical* images, which is why, following St. Augustine, I call them 'archetypes.'"

47. "Archetypes of the Collective Unconscious," *The Archetypes and the Collective Unconscious,* CW 9i, par. 5.

48. Ibid.

49. *C.G. Jung Letters,* vol. 1, p. 329.

50. Ibid., p. 418. Jung expresses much the same in ibid., vol. 2, p. 152.

51. See Jung's major statements on Joachim in *Aion,* CW 9ii, pars. 137ff. Here Jung sketches the mood of the historical period awaiting the Age of the Spirit. He tends to speak sympathetically of Joachim, though indicates that he may well have been "seized by the archetype of the spirit." (Ibid., par. 141)

52. *C.G. Jung Letters,* vol. 2, p. 138.

53. *Aion,* CW 9ii, par. 143: "Some people have rightly seen the Holy Ghost movement as the forerunner of the Reformation."

54. Ibid., par. 155. Jung also refers to the unfortunate reversals paradoxically created by the Spirit movement, in terms he frequently uses to characterize the Enlightenment: "The antichristian era is to blame that the spirit became non-spiritual and that the vitalizing archetype gradually degenerated into rationalism, intellectualism, and doctrinairism, all of which leads straight to the tragedy of modern times now hanging over our heads like a sword of Damocles." (Ibid., par. 141)

55. See Tillich, "The Permanent Significance of the Catholic Church for Protestantism," *Protestant Digest* III (Summer 1941), pp. 23-31; and *Systematic Theology* (Chicago: Chicago University Press, 1963), vol. III, p. 254, where Tillich explicitly relates Protestant principle and Catholic substance.

56. "Psychology and Religion," *Psychology and Religion,* CW 11, par. 17. See also "On the Nature of the Psyche," *The Structure*

and Dynamics of the Psyche, CW 8, par. 405, where Jung speaks of the possessive magic of archetypal powers in these words: "This magic word, which always ends in 'ism,' works most successfully with those who have the least access to their interior selves and have strayed the furthest from their instinctual roots into the truly chaotic world of *collective consciousness.*"

57. That the Portuguese *auto da fé,* used to describe the execution of heretics, translates as "act of the faith," is surely a tribute to the candid character of Portuguese expression.

58. "Answer to Job," *Psychology and Religion,* CW 11, par. 735: "Agnosticism maintains that it does not possess any knowledge of God or of anything metaphysical, overlooking the fact that one never *possesses* a metaphysical belief but is *possessed by it.*"

59. "On the Nature of the Psyche," *The Structure and Dynamics of the Psyche,* CW 8, par. 344: "We are still very far today from Nietzsche's view of philosophy, and indeed of theology, as an "ancilla psychologiae," for not even the psychologist is prepared to regard his statements, at least in part, as a subjectively conditioned confession."

60. In a letter to Hugo Rahner, August 4, 1945, Jung writes: "I only know the one thing I have already pointed out, that Scholastic language and its presuppositions are no longer appropriate for contemporary man if one wants to give him any understanding of the human psyche. I know this not a priori but from repeated experience." (*C.G. Jung Letters,* vol. 1, p. 374)

61. See *Symbols of Transformation,* CW 5, par. 131. Here Jung suggests that St. Francis' stigmata were the result of an identification with Christ; this would be a type of panchristism, similar to the pantheism implicit in Francis' primitive religiosity, where his fellow feeling is grounded both in animal nature and cosmic realities. See also *C.G. Jung Letters,* vol. 1, p. 118.

62. See "Foreword to Suzuki's *Introduction to Zen Buddhism,*" *Psychology and Religion,* CW 11, pars. 887, 893, where Jung compares Eckhart's spirituality to that of the Zen tradition.

63. See, for instance, Jung's reference to Boehme's work in terms of mandala symbolism, which would include the dark side of the deity: "The interpretation of the wheel in Boehme reveals something of the mystical secret of alchemy and is thus of considerable importance in this respect as well as from the psychological point of view: the wheel appears here as a con-

cept for wholeness which represents the essence of mandala symbolism and therefore includes the *mysterium iniquitatis.*" (*Psychology and Alchemy,* CW 12, par. 216)

64. In *Mysterium Coniunctionis,* CW 14, par. 284, Jung cites Silesius's view of God, close to Jung's own reflections on the meaning of the mandala: "God is my centre when I close him in,/And my circumference when I melt in him."

65. See Jung's references to the circular imagery used by Nicholas to express his experience of the unconscious ("Brother Klaus," *Psychology and Religion,* CW 11, par. 484), and to his experience of "the androgyne of the divine ground" (ibid., par. 486).

66. See *C.G. Jung Letters,* vol. 1, p. 540, where he writes to Father Victor White: "I also took a dive into St. Thomas, but I did not feel refreshed afterwards."

67. For evidence of this, see another letter to Father White (ibid., p. 452); a letter to Erich Neumann (ibid., vol. 2, p. 35); and "Psychology and Religion," *Psychology and Religion,* CW 11, par. 161, note 69.

68. See "Paracelsus as a Spiritual Phenomenon," *Alchemical Studies,* CW 13, par. 158, where Jung refers to the *Aurora consurgens* as "falsely ascribed to St. Thomas Aquinas."

Interestingly, however, Jung's co-worker Marie-Louise von Franz, in her series of lectures on alchemy in 1959 at the Zurich Jung Institute, makes a case for Aquinas's authorship of the *Aurora* on the basis of enantiodromia and compensation. (See *Alchemy: An Introduction to the Symbolism and the Psychology,* pp. 177ff.)

69. *Mysterium Coniunctionis,* CW 14, par. 760.

70. "Synchronicity: An Acausal Connecting Principle," *The Structure and Dynamics of the Psyche,* CW 8, par. 926. Interpreting Philo's thought, Jung writes: "Here the great principle or beginning, heaven, is infused into man the microcosm, who reflects the star-like natures and thus, as the smallest part and end of the work of Creation, contains the whole." The same point is made in ibid., par. 929.

71. Ibid., par. 937, note 58. Here Jung acknowledges Wolfgang Pauli as his source for the comparison of Geulincx with Leibnitz. Jung related Leibnitz's conception of "underlying unities" to his own idea of archetypes, and in dialogue with Pauli sought a connection between physics and the collective unconscious.

72. This connection runs throughout Jung's work. It is made explicit in his *Memories, Dreams, Reflections* (pp. 70, 74, 97, 101).

73. "Transformation Symbolism in the Mass," *Psychology and Religion,* CW 11, par. 375.

74. *Psychological Types,* CW 6, par. 512: "What Kant demonstrated in respect of logical thinking is true of the whole range of the psyche."

75. Ibid., par. 659: "The archetype would thus be, to borrow from Kant, the noumenon of the image which intuition perceives and, in perceiving, creates." See also *C.G. Jung Letters,* vol. 2, pp. 572f.

76. See *Two Essays on Analytical Psychology,* CW 7, par. 260, note 7, and *Memories, Dreams, Reflections,* p. 99.

77. Kant, *Religion within the Limits of Reason Alone* (New York: Harper Torchbook, 1960), p. 40.

78. Theodore M. Greene, "The Historical Context and Religious Significance of Kant's *Religion,*" ibid., p. lxvi: "Having consigned his long-loved *Summum Bonum* proof for God's existence, along with the classical proofs which he has demolished in the first *Critique,* to the limbo of false hopes, he now, for the first time in his life, suggests that the moral experience *itself* may legitimately be regarded as an experience of the Divine."

79. Ibid., p. 54. Speaking of the Word as the archetypal instance of moral perfection, Kant writes: "Now it is our universal duty as men to elevate ourselves to this ideal of moral perfection, that is, to the archetype of the moral disposition in all its purity— and for this the idea itself, which reason presents to us for our zealous emulation, can give us power." Kant again uses the word "archetype," in terms of the Christ figure as an image of morally perfect humanity, on pp. 109, 119, 136 and 150.

80. "On the Nature of the Psyche," *The Structure and Dynamics of the Psyche,* CW 8, par. 358: "The victory of Hegel over Kant dealt the gravest blow to reason and to the further development of the German, and, ultimately, of the European mind, all the more dangerous as Hegel was a psychologist in disguise who projected great truths out of the subjective sphere into a cosmos he himself had created." In the next passage Jung joins in the chorus accusing Hegel of "hybris" (ibid., par 359).

81. *C.G. Jung Letters,* vol. 2, p. 501; see also ibid., p. 121, where Jung refers to "the Heideggerean or neo-High German schizophrenic style."

82. Ibid., vol. 1, p. 194.

83. Ibid., vol. 2, p. 502.

84. Ibid., vol. 1, pp. 329 and 328, note 2. Angered that a reviewer had referred to his "romantic vision," Jung writes in reply: "I reject the term 'romantic' for my conception of the unconscious because this is an empirical and anything but a philosophical concept."

85. *Aion,* CW 9ii, par. 11: "If we discount certain suggestive ideas in Leibnitz, Kant, Schelling, and Schopenhauer, and the philosophical excursions of Carus and von Hartmann, it is only since the end of the nineteenth century that modern psychology, with its inductive methods, has discovered the foundations of consciousness and proved empirically the existence of a psyche outside consciousness."

86. See *Psychological Types,* CW 6, par. 59, where Jung locates Anselm within "the psychological disposition of realism in general." Commenting on the ontological argument, he writes: "The real point is that it is a psychological fact whose existence and efficacy are so overwhelmingly clear that no sort of argumentation is needed to prove it." (Ibid., par. 62) Though this is written of Anselm's position, it is not far from Jung's own.

87. Jung writes that even in his youth he already felt the experience of God to be endemic to his consciousness and to humanity's, when not blocked by bad theology. Recalling dialogues with his minister father: "I saw that my critical questions made him sad, but I nevertheless hoped for a constructive talk, since it appeared almost inconceivable to me that he should not have had experience of God, the most evident of all experiences. I knew enough about epistemology to realize that knowledge of this sort could not be proved, but it was equally clear to me that it stood in no more need of proof than the beauty of a sunset or the terrors of the night." (*Memories, Dreams, Reflections,* p. 92)

88. *C.G. Jung Letters,* vol. 1, p. 332. Jung adds: "I would have said to Kierkegaard straight off: 'God is straightway with you and is the voice within you.'"

89. Ibid., vol. 2, p. 145. Regine Olsen was the woman Kierkegaard professed to love but forsook. The editors of Jung's letters explain in a footnote: "Jung's use of the Latinized form 'Regina' is an allusion to the alchemical *opus* or, psychologically, the process of individuation, in which the partnership of Rex (king = animus) and Regina (queen = anima) is essential for its completion."

90. See *Psychology and Alchemy,* CW 12, par. 11, note 6, where

Jung writes that it is "psychologically quite unthinkable for God to be simply the 'wholly other,' for a 'wholly other' could never be one of the soul's deepest and closest intimacies—which is precisely what God is."

91. Tillich, *Systematic Theology* (Chicago: Chicago University Press, 1963), vol. 3, p. 421.

92. Teilhard de Chardin, "Panthéism et christianism," *Comment Je Crois,* Oeuvres de Pierre Teilhard de Chardin (Paris: Editions du Seuil, 1969), vol. 10, pp. 71-93. See also the references to pantheism in the 1924 version of "Mons univers," *Science et Christ,* ibid., vol. 9, pp. 87, 114.

93. *Enchiridion Symbolorum,* ed. Henricus Denzinger (Rome: Herder, 1964), nos. 3023-3025, p. 593.

94. For a recent discussion of this issue see John T. Ford's article in *Religious Studies Review,* vol. 8, no. 4 (October 1982), pp. 342f.

95. Denzinger, *Enchiridion Symbolorum,* nos. 3135-3140, pp. 610-612.

96. Ibid., no. 3004, p. 588.

97. See *C.G. Jung Letters,* vol. 2, p. 115, where Jung refers to Schleiermacher as "really one of my spiritual ancestors."

98. "Psychology and Religion," *Psychology and Religion,* CW 11, par. 9.

99. *Aion,* CW 9ii, par. 76.

100. See "A Psychological Approach to the Dogma of the Trinity," *Psychology and Religion,* CW 11; and "Christ, a Symbol of the Self," *Aion,* CW 9ii.

101. "A Psychological Approach to the Dogma of the Trinity," *Psychology and Religion,* CW 11, pars. 172-193.

102. Ibid., pars. 197ff.

103. Ibid., pars. 222-242.

104. "Transformation Symbolism in the Mass," ibid., pars. 296-396.

105. Ibid., par. 414: "The mystery of the Eucharist transforms the soul of the empirical man, who is only part of himself, into his totality, symbolically expressed by Christ. In this sense, therefore, we can speak of the *rite of the individuation process.*"

106. Ibid., pars. 397-448. Typically, Jung writes: "What nevertheless drives us to it [becoming more conscious] is the self, which demands sacrifice by sacrificing itself to us." (Ibid., par. 400)

107. Ibid., par. 395.

108. "A Psychological Approach to the Dogma of the Trinity," ibid., pars. 243-285.

109. "Answer to Job," ibid., par. 575. The religious and psychological implications of Jung's work on the Job legend are developed at length in Edward F. Edinger, *The Creation of Consciousness: Jung's Myth for Modern Man* (Toronto: Inner City Books, 1984).

110. "Answer to Job," *Psychology and Religion,* CW 11, par. 642.

111. Ibid., par. 647.

112. "A Psychological Approach to the Dogma of the Trinity," ibid., par. 252.

113. Jung seems early on to have perceived the unfortunate consequences of an unnaturally spiritualized view of the feminine, as presented in the image of the Virgin Mary, particularly the hostility this breeds toward real women. In 1921 he writes: "And since all unconscious contents, when activated by dissociated libido, are projected upon external objects, the devaluation of the real woman was compensated by daemonic traits. She no longer appeared as an object of love but as a persecutor or witch. The consequence of increasing Mariolatry was the witch hunt, that indelible blot on the later Middle Ages." (*Psychological Types,* CW 6, par. 399)

114. Denzinger, *Enchiridion Symbolorum,* nos. 1701-2980, pp. 576-584.

115. Ibid., nos. 3875-3899, pp. 772-780.

116. "Psychological Aspects of the Mother Archetype," *The Archetypes and the Collective Unconscious,* CW 9i, par. 190. Jung goes on to quote Buri citing Bultmann, implying that humanity is no longer capable of considering itself as the object of invasion by "alien forces." Jung locates these forces in the unconscious and gives to them just such invasive powers. In a similar vein, he warns about demythologizing the Christ figure and taking his sayings on the level of personal psychology. In Jung's estimate this would turn the historical Jesus into a man possessed or "beside himself." ("Answer to Job," *Psychology and Religion,* CW 11, par. 647)

117. *C.G. Jung Letters,* vol. 2, p. 9.

118. Ibid., vol. 1, p. 567.

119. Paradoxically, this may be just the point Jung himself makes in his earlier evaluation of Marian doctrine and its relation to medieval witch-hunting (above, note 113).

120. See note 113.

121. See especially Jung's letter of November 24, 1953 (*C.G. Jung*

Letters, vol. 2, pp. 133ff). References to the debate with White are also scattered throughout Jung's *Collected Works.* A succinct statement of Jung's position is to be found in *Aion,* CW 9ii, par. 112, note 74.

122. One of Jung's best formulations of this problem is in "A Psychological Approach to the Dogma of the Trinity," *Psychology and Religion,* CW 11, par. 247.

123. This is one of the central points in Jung's "Answer to Job."

124. "A Psychological Approach to the Dogma of the Trinity," ibid., par. 258.

125. The opposition between Christ and Satan is only one manifestation of the archetype of the hostile brothers, which according to Jung is constellated in any conflict situation (ibid., pars. 254ff). Psychologically it relates to the conflict between ego and shadow.

126. "Answer to Job," ibid., par. 739: "The mediation between the opposites was already indicated in the symbolism of Christ's fate, in the crucifixion scene where the mediator hangs between two thieves, one of whom goes to paradise, the other down to hell." Jung goes on to refer to the symbolism of this scene as pointing ultimately to the resolution of "the antinomy in Deity itself" (ibid).

127. *C.G. Jung Letters,* vol. 2, p. 136.

128. Ibid., p. 137.

129. This is a basic theme in Jung's critique of the Christ image. It is put succinctly in "Christ, a Symbol of the Self," *Aion,* CW 9ii, par. 74, where Jung writes: "There can be no doubt that the original Christian conception of the *imago Dei* embodied in Christ meant an all-embracing totality that even includes the animal side of man."

130. "Gnostic Symbols of the Self," ibid., par. 314.

131. Seen from Mary's standpoint, the story is a psychologem applicable to women, for the vision of Jesus splitting into male and female serves to compensate a pure, deified view of a wholly masculine Christ. (Ibid., par. 320)

132. See Lucy Menzies, trans., *The Revelations of Mechthilde von Magdeburg: The Flowing Light of the Godhead* (London: Longmans, Green, 1953).

133. Julian of Norwich, *Revelations of Divine Love,* trans. Clifton Wolters (Baltimore: Penguin Books, 1966), p. 166. Julian

writes: "In our Mother, Christ, we grow and develop. . . . " Like Mechthilde of Magdeburg, Julian also depicts the relation between the Trinity and the human in terms of sexual love: "In this uniting together he is our real, true husband, and we his loved wife and sweetheart. He is never displeased with his wife!" (Ibid., p. 165)

134. "The Psychology of the Transference," *The Practice of Psychotherapy,* CW 16, par. 525.

135. Jacob Boehme, *The Way to Christ,* trans. Peter Erb (New York: Paulist Press, 1978), nos. 45-51, pp. 57-62.

136. "Psychological Commentary on *The Tibetan Book of the Great Liberation,"* *Psychology and Religion,* CW 11, par. 787.

137. *Memories, Dreams, Reflections,* p. 378: "The dead came back from Jerusalem, where they found not what they sought."

138. For a typical example, see "Psychological Commentary on *The Tibetan Book of the Dead,"* *Psychology and Religion,* CW 11, par. 840: "No sun is thereby eclipsed for the Oriental as it would be for the Christian, who would feel robbed of his God; on the contrary, his soul [the Oriental's] is the light of the Godhead and the Godhead is the soul."

139. *Psychology and Alchemy,* CW 12, pars. 9 10.

140. "The Phenomenology of the Spirit in Fairytales," *The Archetypes and the Collective Unconscious,* CW 9i, par. 454. Jung goes on to say that "former ages did not exaggerate . . . the spirit has not sloughed off its demonisms. . . . True, the archetype of the spirit is capable of working for good as well as for evil, but it depends on man's free—i.e., conscious—decision whether the good also will be perverted into something satanic. Man's worst sin is unconsciousness, but it is indulged with the greatest piety even by those who should serve mankind as teachers and examples." (Ibid., par. 455)

141. "On the Nature of the Psyche," *The Structure and Dynamics of the Psyche,* CW 8, par. 427.

142. "A Study in the Process of Individuation," *The Archetypes and the Collective Unconscious,* CW 9i, par. 542. See also "Concerning Mandala Symbolism," ibid., pars. 627ff, and "Commentary on *The Secret of the Golden Flower,"* *Alchemical Studies,* CW 13.

143. "Psychology and Religion," *Psychology and Religion,* CW 11, par. 141.

144. Ibid.

145. Ibid., par. 105: "Though we have the logion 'I and the Father are one, who seeth me seeth the Father,' it would be considered blasphemy or madness to stress Christ's dogmatic humanity to such a degree that man would identify himself with Christ and his homoousia. But this is precisely what seems to be meant by the symbol. . . . The Church, it seems to me, probably has to repudiate any attempt to take such conclusions seriously. She may even have to condemn any approach to these experiences, since she cannot admit that nature unites what she herself [the Church] has divided."

146. Hence Jung's view, already noted (page 48) that a neurosis is never cured, especially in the second half of life, without the development or rediscovery of a religious attitude, i.e., "an experience of the *numinosum.*" (See above, note 98)

147. See *Aion,* CW 9ii, par. 170, where Jung contends that images of God and of the Self are indistinguishable, adding that "*the destruction of the God-image is followed by the annulment of the personality.*" (Jung's italics)

148. Ibid., par. 125.

149. "Psychotherapy or the Clergy," *Psychology and Religion,* CW 11, par. 511.

150. Ibid., par. 512.

151. Tillich, *Systematic Theology,* vol. 1, p. 139.

152. See "The Symbolic Life," *The Symbolic Life,* CW 18, par. 671. Here Jung writes of those people who can lead an adequate spiritual life within the Church: "They have no right to be neurotic. They belong to a Church, and if you can help them to slip back to the Church you have helped them. Several of my patients became Catholics, others went back into the Church organization."

153. Ibid., par. 618: "When a practising Catholic comes to me, I say, 'Did you confess this to your father-confessor?'"

154. Ibid., par. 609: "In my forty years of experience I have had no more than six practising Catholics among my patients."

155. See "On Psychic Energy," *The Structure and Dynamics of the Psyche,* CW 8, par. 110. Jung goes on: "For a long time and for the great majority of mankind the symbol of a collective religion will suffice. It is perhaps only temporarily and for relatively few individuals that the existing collective religions have become inadequate." (Ibid., par. 111)

156. Jung suggests that the tension arising between one's individual religious truth and that of the collective is responsible for

cultural progress: "Every advance in culture.... begins with individuation, that is to say with the individual.... If he succeeds in giving collective validity to his widened consciousness, he creates a tension of opposites that provides the stimulation which culture needs for its further progress." (Ibid.)

157. Jung twice deals with Pauli's material: in the series of dreams that is the substance of his work, "Individual Dream Symbolism in Relation to Alchemy," *Psychology and Alchemy,* CW 12; and in his discussion of particular dreams of Pauli's in "Psychology and Religion," *Psychology and Religion,* CW 11, pars. 40ff.

158. Jung interprets a central dream of Pauli's variously as representing "an attempt to seek refuge ... in the shelter of a church religion" (ibid., par. 56), and as a "cheap compromise" (ibid., par. 71).

159. "Any contact with the unconscious that goes at all deep leads to transference phenomena," writes Jung. "Whenever, therefore, the clergyman penetrates any distance into the psychic background, he will provoke a transference (with men as well as with women)." ("Psychoanalysis and the Cure of Souls," *Psychology and Religion,* CW 11, par. 549) Such situations are exceedingly difficult to understand and to deal with, especially without a thorough personal analysis.

160. "Transformation Symbolism in the Mass," ibid., par. 444.

161. "A Psychological Approach to the Dogma of the Trinity," ibid., par. 295. A succinct statement of Jung's critical appreciation of Christianity is also to be found in "Christ, a Symbol of the Self," *Aion,* CW 9ii, par. 79: "It is ... well to examine carefully the psychological aspects of the individuation process in the light of Christian tradition, which can describe it for us with an exactness and impressiveness far surpassing our feeble attempts, even though the Christian image of the self—Christ—lacks the shadow that properly belongs to it."

162. "Transformation Symbolism in the Mass," *Psychology and Religion,* CW 11, par. 445.

163. Tillich, *Systematic Theology,* vol. 1, pp. 95f: "This is the knowledge of which Paul also speaks, the *gnosis* which in New Testament Greek means cognitive, sexual, and mystical union at the same time. In this respect there is no contrast between Socrates and Paul." The connection between *gnosis* and *amor intellectualis* is made in ibid., pp. 153f.

164. *Memories, Dreams, Reflections,* p. 62.

165. Ibid., p. 42. Again referring to his father, Jung writes: "But he did not know of the immediate living God who stands, omnipotent and free, who calls upon man to partake of His freedom, and can force him to renounce his own views and convictions in order to fulfill without reserve the command of God." (Ibid., p. 40)

166. *Mysterium Coniunctionis,* CW 14, par. 742.

167. Ibid.

168. Ibid., par. 747: "Had the alchemists not had at least a secret premonition that their Christian *unio mentalis* had not yet realized the union with the world of the body, their almost mystical thirst for knowledge would scarcely be explicable, let alone the symbolism, rivalling that of Christianity, which began to develop already at the end of the thirteenth century."

169. Ibid., par. 760.

Index

Age of the Spirit, 35-36, 57-58,
   64-65
agnosticism, 106
alchemy, 32-34, 40-42, 95, 97-99,
   106, 109, 116
amor intellectualis, 95, 115
analytic psychology: and
   religion, 7-12, 23-25, 83-92
   and compensation, 13-14
ancillae psychologiae, 38, 106
androgyny, 68, 99, 107, 112
anima, 66-67, 109
animus, 67, 109
Anselm, St., 47
Anthropos, 10
Aquinas, Thomas, 33, 41, 49
archetypal possession, 12, 26, 39-
   40, 78-79, 105-106
archetype(s): 7, 10, 23, 37-38, 43-
   44, 104-105, 107-108
   numinosity of, 23-24, 28,
      35, 44-45, 50, 55
   of Self, 31
   use of term, 34-35, 43-45,
      108
Aristotle/Aristotelian, 32-33, 39,
   41, 103
asceticism, 97-98
Assumption of Mary, 58-62, 102
atheism, 19, 33, 75, 104
atonement, 53
Augustine, 32, 34
Aurora consurgens, 41
auto-da-fé, 38

Barth, Karl, 48
Black Madonna, 62
body, and spirit, 29-30, 65-68,
   94, 97-100

Boehme, Jacob, 40, 68
Bonaventure, 34, 39, 77
Buddha, 10
Bultmann, Rudolf, 59

capitalism, 37, 81
Carus, 43
Catholicism, 16-17, 20, 36, 48-62,
   89-91, 96-97, 114
chastity, 67
Christ: androgynous, 68, 112
   and Dionysus, 104
   as essential humanity, 30
   in Gnosticism, 94-96
   as historical figure, 10, 51-
      52, 81, 95, 111
   imitation of, 66
   Incarnation of, 56-57, 68
   and Mercurius, 33-34, 97
   and Satan, 62-66, 112
   and sexuality, 65-68
   as Self, 10, 35, 115
   as symbol, 10, 30, 33-35,
      51-69, 80-81, 110-112,
      114-115
Christianity: 14-21
   and analytic psychology, 7-
      12, 24, 83-92
   compensation for, 29-34,
      62, 65, 93-100
   and evil, 62-68
   feminine in, 58-62, 111
   and fishes (Pisces), 29
   ideal, 36
   and illness, 9, 12, 14-15, 21,
      30, 50-69, 73, 91-92, 99-
      100
   Jung's ambivalence toward,
      7-12, 21, 23, 29, 51

117

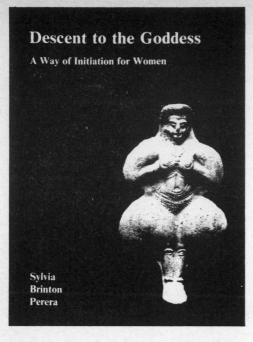

Descent to the Goddess

A Way of Initiation for Women

Sylvia
Brinton
Perera

6. Descent to the Goddess: A Way of Initiation for Women. $10
Sylvia Brinton Perera (New York). ISBN 0-919123-05-8. 112 pages.

This is a highly original and provocative book about women's freedom and the need for an inner, female authority in a masculine-oriented society.

Combining ancient texts and modern dreams, the author, a practising therapist, presents a way of feminine initiation. Inanna-Ishtar, Sumerian Goddess of Heaven and Earth, journeys into the underworld to Ereshkigal, her dark "sister," and returns. So modern women must descend from their old role-determined behavior into the depths of their instinct and image patterns, to find anew the Great Goddess and restore her values to modern culture.

Men too will be interested in this book, both for its revelations of women's essential nature and for its implications in terms of their own inner journey.

"The most significant contribution to an understanding of feminine psychology since Esther Harding's *Way of All Women.*"—**Marion Woodman,** psychoanalyst and author of *The Owl Was a Baker's Daughter.*

Addiction to Perfection
The Still Unravished Bride

A Psychological Study by
Marion Woodman

12. Addiction to Perfection: The Still Unravished Bride.
Marion Woodman (Toronto). ISBN 0-919123-11-2. 208 pages. $12

"This book is about taking the head off an evil witch." With these words Marion Woodman begins her spiral journey, a powerful and authoritative look at the psychology and attitudes of modern woman.

The witch is a Medusa or a Lady Macbeth, an archetypal pattern functioning autonomously in women, petrifying their spirit and inhibiting their development as free and creatively receptive individuals. Much of this, according to the author, is due to a cultural one-sidedness that favors patriarchal values—productivity, goal orientation, intellectual excellence, spiritual perfection, etc.—at the expense of more earthy, interpersonal values that have traditionally been recognized as the heart of the feminine.

Marion Woodman's first book, *The Owl Was a Baker's Daughter: Obesity, Anorexia Nervosa and the Repressed Feminine,* focused on the psychology of eating disorders and weight disturbances.

Here, with a broader perspective on the same general themes, Marion Woodman continues her remarkable exploration of women's mysteries through case material, dreams, literature and mythology, in food rituals, rape symbolism, Christianity, imagery in the body, sexuality, creativity and relationships.

The final chapter, a discussion of the psychological meaning of ravishment (as opposed to rape), celebrates the integration of body and spirit and shows what this can mean to a woman in terms of her personal independence.

Studies in Jungian Psychology
by Jungian Analysts

LIMITED EDITION PAPERBACKS

Prices quoted are in U.S. dollars (except for Canadian orders)

1. The Secret Raven: Conflict and Transformation.
Daryl Sharp (Toronto). ISBN 0-919123-00-7. 128 pages. $10

A concise introduction to the application of Jungian psychology. Focuses on the creative personality—and the life and dreams of the writer Franz Kafka —but the psychology is relevant to anyone who has experienced a conflict between the spiritual life and sex, or between inner and outer reality. (Knowledge of Kafka is not necessary.) Illustrated. Bibliography.

2. The Psychological Meaning of Redemption Motifs in Fairytales.
Marie-Louise von Franz (Zurich). ISBN 0-919123-01-5. 128 pages. $10

A unique account of the significance of fairytales for an understanding of the process of individuation, especially in terms of integrating animal nature and human nature. Particularly helpful for its symbolic, nonlinear approach to the meaning of typical dream motifs (bathing, beating, clothes, animals, etc.), and its clear description of complexes and projection.

3. On Divination and Synchronicity: Psychology of Meaningful Chance.
Marie-Louise von Franz (Zurich). ISBN 0-919123-02-3. 128 pages. $10

A penetrating study of the meaning of the irrational. Examines time, number, and methods of divining fate such as the I Ching, astrology, Tarot, palmistry, random patterns, etc. Explains Jung's ideas on archetypes, projection, psychic energy and synchronicity, contrasting Western scientific attitudes with those of the Chinese and so-called primitives. Illustrated.

4. The Owl Was a Baker's Daughter: Obesity, Anorexia Nervosa, and the Repressed Feminine.
Marion Woodman (Toronto). ISBN 0-919123-03-1. 144 pages. $10

A pioneer work in feminine psychology, with particular attention to the body as mirror of the psyche in eating disorders and weight disturbances. Explores the personal and cultural loss—and potential rediscovery—of the feminine principle, through Jung's Association Experiment, case studies, dreams, Christianity and mythology. Illustrated. Glossary. Bibliography.

5. Alchemy: An Introduction to the Symbolism and the Psychology.
Marie-Louise von Franz (Zurich). ISBN 0-919123-04-X. 288 pages. $16

A lucid and practical guide to what the alchemists were really looking for— emotional balance and wholeness. Completely demystifies the subject. An important work, invaluable for an understanding of images and motifs in modern dreams and drawings, and indispensable for anyone interested in relationships and communication between the sexes. 84 Illustrations.

6. Descent to the Goddess: A Way of Initiation for Women.
Sylvia Brinton Perera (New York). ISBN 0-919123-05-8. 112 pages. $10

A timely and provocative study of women's freedom and the need for an inner, female authority in a masculine-oriented society. Based on the Sumerian goddess Inanna-Ishtar's journey to the underworld, her transformation through contact with her dark "sister" Ereshkigal, and her return. Rich in insights from dreams, mythology and analysis. Glossary. Bibliography.

7. **The Psyche as Sacrament: C.G. Jung and Paul Tillich.**
   John P. Dourley (Ottawa). ISBN 0-919123-06-6. 128 pages. $10

An illuminating, comparative study showing with great clarity that in the depths of the soul the psychological task and the religious task are one. With a dual perspective, the author—Jungian analyst and Catholic priest—examines the deeper meaning, for Christian and non-Christian alike, of God, Christ, the Spirit, the Trinity, morality and the religious life. Glossary.

8. **Border Crossings: Carlos Castaneda's Path of Knowledge.**
   Donald Lee Williams (Boulder). ISBN 0-919123-07-4. 160 pages. $12

The first thorough psychological examination of the popular don Juan novels. Using dreams, fairytales, and mythic and cultural parallels, the author brings Castaneda's spiritual journey down to earth, in terms of everyone's search for self-realization. Special attention to the psychology of women. (Familiarity with the novels is not necessary.) Glossary.

9. **Narcissism and Character Transformation: The Psychology of Narcissistic Character Disorders.**
   Nathan Schwartz-Salant (New York). ISBN 0-919123-08-2. 192 pp. $13

An incisive and comprehensive analysis of narcissism: what it looks like, what it means and how to deal with it. Shows how an understanding of the archetypal patterns that underlie the individual, clinical symptoms of narcissism can point the way to a healthy restructuring of the personality. Draws upon a variety of psychoanalytic points of view (Jungian, Freudian, Kohutian, Kleinian, etc.). Illustrated. Glossary. Bibliography.

10. **Rape and Ritual: A Psychological Study.**
    Bradley A. Te Paske (Minneapolis). ISBN 0-919123-09-0. 160 pp. $12

An absorbing combination of theory, clinical material, dreams and mythology, penetrating far beyond the actual deed to the impersonal, archetypal background of sexual assault. Special attention to male ambivalence toward women and the psychological significance of rape dreams and fantasies. Illustrated. Glossary. Bibliography.

11. **Alcoholism and Women: The Background and the Psychology.**
    Jan Bauer (Zurich). ISBN 0-919123-10-4. 144 pages. $12

A major contribution to an understanding of alcoholism, particularly in women. Compares and contrasts medical and psychological models, illustrates the relative merits of Alcoholics Anonymous and individual therapy, and presents new ways of looking at the problem based on case material, dreams and archetypal patterns. Glossary. Bibliography.

12. **Addiction to Perfection: The Still Unravished Bride.**
    Marion Woodman (Toronto). ISBN 0-919123-11-2. 208 pages. $12

A powerful and authoritative look at the psychology and attitudes of modern woman, expanding on the themes introduced in *The Owl Was a Baker's Daughter*. Explores the nature of the feminine through case material, dreams and mythology, in food rituals, rape symbolism, perfectionism, imagery in the body, sexuality and creativity. Illustrated.

13. **Jungian Dream Interpretation: A Handbook of Theory and Practice.**
    James A. Hall, M.D. (Dallas). ISBN 0-919123-12-0. 128 pages. $12

A comprehensive and practical guide to an understanding of dreams in light of the basic concepts of Jungian psychology. Jung's model of the psyche is described and discussed, with many clinical examples. Particular attention to common dream motifs, and how dreams are related to the stage of life and individuation process of the dreamer. Glossary.

14. **The Creation of Consciousness: Jung's Myth for Modern Man.**
Edward F. Edinger, M.D. (Los Angeles). ISBN 0-919123-13-9. 128 pages. $12

An important new book by the author of *Ego and Archetype,* proposing a new world-view based on a creative collaboration between the scientific pursuit of knowledge and the religious search for meaning. Explores the significance for mankind of Jung's life and work; discusses the purpose of human life and what it means to be conscious; examines the theological and psychological implications of Jung's master-work, *Answer to Job;* presents a radical, psychological understanding of God's "continuing incarnation"; and illustrates the pressing need for man to become more conscious of his dark, destructive side as well as his creative potential. Illustrated.

15. **The Analytic Encounter: Transference and Human Relationship.**
Mario Jacoby (Zurich). ISBN 0-919123-14-7. 128 pages. $12

A sensitive and revealing study that differentiates relationships based on projection from those characterized by psychological distance and mutual respect. Examines the psychodynamics activated in any intimate relationship, and particularly in therapy and analysis; summarizes the views of Jung and Freud on identification, projection and transference-countertransference, as well as those of Martin Buber (I-It and I-Thou relationships); and shows how unconscious complexes may appear in dreams and emotional reactions. Special attention to the so-called narcissistic transferences (mirror, idealizing, etc.), the archetypal roots of projection and the significance of erotic love in the analytic situation. Glossary. Bibliography.

16. **Change of Life: A Psychological Study of the Menopause.**
Ann Mankowitz (Santa Fe). ISBN 0-919123-15-5. 128 pages. $12

A detailed and profoundly moving account of a menopausal woman's Jungian analysis, openly facing the fears and apprehensions behind the collective "conspiracy of silence" that surrounds this crucial period of every woman's life. Dramatically interweaves the experience of one woman with more generally applicable social, biological, emotional and psychological factors; frankly discusses the realities of aging, within which the menopause is seen as a potentially creative rite of passage; and illustrates how the menopause may manifest, both in outer life and in dreams, as a time of rebirth, an opportunity for psychological integration and growth, increased strength and wisdom. Glossary. Bibliography.

All books contain detailed Index

INNER CITY BOOKS
Box 1271, Station Q, Toronto, Canada M4T 2P4
(416) 927-0355

ORDER FORM

Please detach and fill out both sides
Prices quoted are in U.S. dollars
(except for Canadian orders)

Title	Price	Copies	Amount
1. Raven	$10	_____	_____
2. Redemption	$10	_____	_____
3. Divination	$10	_____	_____
4. The Owl	$10	_____	_____
5. Alchemy	$16	_____	_____
6. Descent	$10	_____	_____
7. Psyche	$10	_____	_____
8. Border	$12	_____	_____
9. Narcissism	$13	_____	_____
10. Rape	$12	_____	_____
11. Alcoholism	$12	_____	_____
12. Addiction	$12	_____	_____
13. Dream	$12	_____	_____
14. Creation	$12	_____	_____
15. Encounter	$12	_____	_____
16. Change	$12	_____	_____

Subtotal: _____

Less Discount if applicable: _____

Or Plus Postage/Handling (80¢ per book): _____

TOTAL: _____

Orders from outside Canada pay in $U.S.

Make check or money order payable to **INNER CITY BOOKS**

REMARKS